THE ORMESBY PSALTER

The Ormesby Psalter

Patrons & Artists in Medieval East Anglia

FREDERICA C.E. LAW-TURNER

Bodleian Library
UNIVERSITY OF OXFORD

First published in 2017 by
the Bodleian Library
Broad Street, Oxford OX1 3BG

www.bodleianshop.co.uk

ISBN   978 1 85124 310 5

Text © Frederica C.E. Law-Turner, 2017

Images, unless specified on pp. 157–60
© Bodleian Library, University of Oxford, 2017

All rights reserved

No part of this book may be reproduced, stored in a retrieval system, or transmitted in any form or by any means, electronic, mechanical, photocopying, recording, or otherwise, without the written permission of the Bodleian Library, except for the purpose of research or private study, or criticism or review.

Cover design by Dot Little at the Bodleian Library
Designed and typeset by illuminati
in 11½ on 16 Monotype Bembo

Printed and bound by Great Wall Printing Co. Ltd,
Hong Kong on 157gsm Chen Ming matt art

British Library Catalogue in Publishing Data
A CIP record of this publication is available from the British Library

CONTENTS

ACKNOWLEDGEMENTS — vii
MAP — ix
FAMILY TREES — x

INTRODUCTION — 1

Modern history 3
Medieval owners 4
The book as a book 6
The puzzle 8
Making the Ormesby Psalter 13
The late-thirteenth-century campaign 15
The 1310s campaign 25
The Jesse Master 29
The Ormesby Master 45
The 1330s campaign 83
The Earl of Ufford and the final campaign 96
Conclusion 100

DESCRIPTIVE COMMENTARY — 103

Psalm 1, *Beatus vir* 105
Psalm 1, *Beatus vir* 108
Psalm 26, *Dominus illuminatio mea* 110
Psalm 38, *Dixi custodiam vias meas* 113
Psalm 51, *Quid gloriaris in malitia* 117
Psalm 52, *Dixit insipiens* 119
Psalm 68, *Salvum me fac deus* 122
Psalm 80, *Exultate Deo* 125
Psalm 97, *Cantate domino* 128
Psalm 101, *Domine exaudi orationem meam* 131
Psalm 109, *Dixit dominus domino meo* 135

APPENDIX	137
NOTES	146
SUGGESTED READING	151
LIST OF ILLUSTRATIONS	157
INDEX	161

ACKNOWLEDGEMENTS

I have known the Ormesby Psalter for over twenty years. It first came to my attention in 1994 when it was the subject of my M.A. dissertation at the Courtauld Institute of Art in London. I went on to write my Ph.D. there on the manuscript, under the patient supervision of John Lowden FBA, Professor of Mediaeval Art History at the Courtauld. The task of turning part of my thesis into this book and a forthcoming article has taken longer than initially anticipated and my ideas on the manuscript have developed considerably. Many people have generously contributed advice and assistance. I owe a particular debt of gratitude to Martin Kauffmann, Head of Early and Rare Collections and Tolkien Curator of Medieval Manuscripts at the Bodleian Library, for his unwavering support throughout this project, for the unparalleled access which he has allowed to one of the Bodleian's greatest treasures, and for his helpful comments on previous drafts of this text. I have also benefited enormously from discussions with François Avril, Michelle Brown, Michael Michael, David King, Lucy Sandler, Alison Stones and Stella Panayotova. Especial thanks are owed to Michael Gullick for his examination and illuminating discussion of the binding, to Alison Stones for access to her as then unpublished articles and catalogue descriptions of the de Bar manuscripts, to Kay Davenport for her de Bar genealogies, and to Roger Wieck and Jane Lattes of the Morgan Library for reading a draft version of this text. Any errors are entirely my own.

Thanks are also due to the staff of the many libraries around the world who have allowed access to their manuscripts and reference material, including the Bodleian Library, Oxford; the British Library, London; the Bibliothèque nationale de France, Paris; the Bibliothèques municipales at Douai, Metz and Verdun;

Emmanuel College, Trinity College and the Fitzwilliam Museum, Cambridge; the Watson Library at the Metropolitan Museum of Art, the Cloisters Library and the Morgan Library, New York; New York Public Library; Norwich Castle Museum, Norwich; the Society of Antiquaries, London; and Trinity College Dublin, among others. Thanks also go to English Heritage; the Dean and Chapter of Norwich Cathedral; the Norfolk Archaeological Trust; the churchwardens of St Margaret's Cley-next-the-Sea, St Mary's Elsing, St Mary's Gressenhall and St Peter's Ringland in Norfolk, St Mary's Thornham Parva, Suffolk, and St Peter's Lowick, Northamptonshire. My thanks to Charles Sainsbury-Plaice for his wonderful photographs of the churches and buildings of Norfolk, and to Roger Rosewell for his images of the glass in St Peter's Lowick.

The British Academy provided a grant for travel and for photography for this book. Thanks are also due to Samuel Fanous, to the editorial team at Bodleian Library Publishing, and finally to my family for their unflagging support over many years.

All biblical quotations and their translations are taken from the Douay-Rheims translation of the Vulgate. For the sake of consistency, I have retained Sidney Cockerell's system of sections rather than quires, as used in the Roxburghe Club volume, *Two East Anglian Psalters at the Bodleian Library* (Oxford, 1926), which remains the most important publication on the Ormesby Psalter to date. Each section equates to a quire, but Section 1 begins at fol. 10, the first quire of the original core of the manuscript.

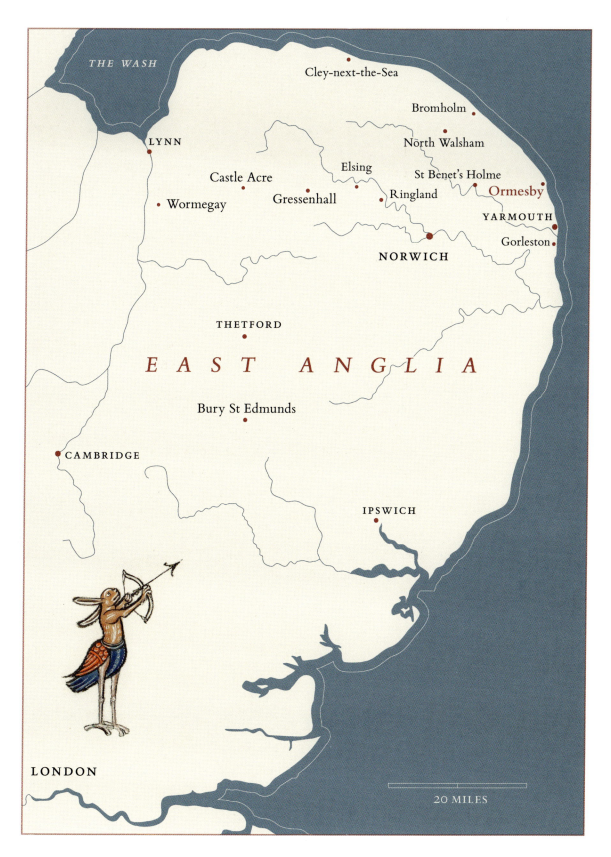

MEDIEVAL EAST ANGLIA

THE BARDOLFS OF WORMEGAY

Thomas BARDOLF   Reginald de WARENNE
d. 1188/94

Doun d. 1205   m.   Beatrice d. 1214

William d. 1275/6
m. Nichola

William d. 1289
m. Juliana de Gurnay d. 1295

Hugh 1259–1303/4   Thomas
1ST BARON BARDOLF   d. *before* 1327
m. Isabella Aguillon d. *c.*1323   m. Cecily

Thomas 1282–1328   William d. 1324   Margery   Joan
2ND BARON BARDOLF
m. Agnes de Grandson d. 1357

John 1311–1363   Cecily d. 1388   + other children
3rd BARON BARDOLF   m. 1st Robert de Yelverton
m. Elizabeth d'Amory   m. 2nd William 3rd Lord Morley

their heirs   *their heirs*

THE FOLIOTS OF GRESSENHALL

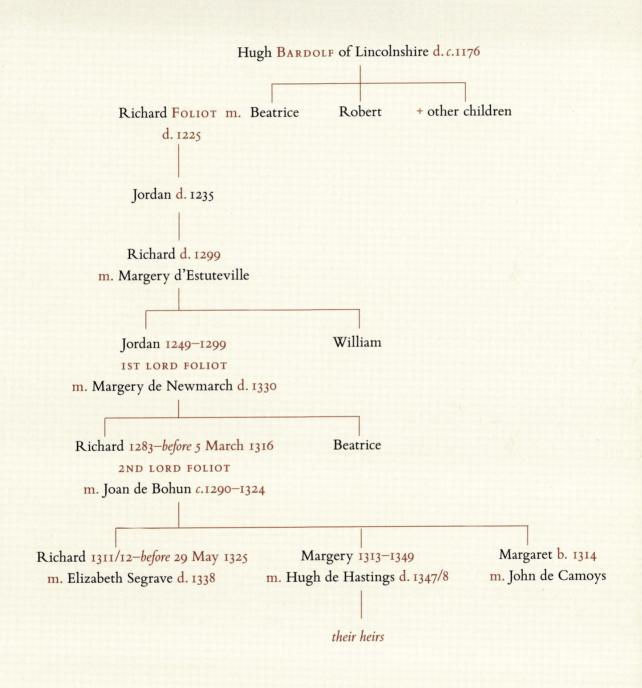

The Ormesby Psalter

INTRODUCTION

Salterium fratris Roberti de Or
mesby monachi Norwyci per eundē
assignatū choro ecclie sce Trinitatis
Norwici ad iacendū coram Supiore
qui pro tempore fuerit in perpetuum.

> The Psalter of brother Robert of Ormesby, monk
> of Norwich, assigned by him to the choir of the
> church of the Holy Trinity of Norwich to lie in
> the place of the subprior for all time.

The manuscript containing this inscription is one of the most
magnificent yet enigmatic of the great Gothic psalters written
and illuminated in England in the first half of the fourteenth
century. Now among the greatest treasures of the Bodleian
Library, it takes its name from Robert of Ormesby, subprior at
Norwich Cathedral Priory in the 1330s, whose donation of the
book to his community is recorded in red at the beginning of
the manuscript (FIGURE 1).[1]

Modern history

The Psalter came to the Bodleian in 1834 as part of the bequest
of Francis Douce (1757–1834), the former Keeper of Manuscripts
at the British Museum. Douce purchased it in November 1831
from the London rare books and manuscripts dealer Thomas
Thorpe, an acquisition recorded with characteristic terseness
in his accession book for that year: 'Fine Norwich psalter.
Thorpe'.[2] Nothing is known of how or where Thorpe found the
book, although it may well have remained at Norwich until the
dissolution of the Cathedral Priory on 2 May 1538, and possibly
for some time after. The erasure of the name of Thomas Becket
and the word *pape* (pope) in the Calendar suggests that the
manuscript was still in use by the time of Edward VI's suppres-
sion of religious books in 1547. Norwich was one of the eight
cathedral priories that were to continue as secular cathedrals,
and was refounded immediately under the management of a
dean and chapter. Many Norwich manuscripts migrated to
Cambridge in the second half of the sixteenth century, but the
Ormesby Psalter was not among them. The inscription 'A. Gray'

1 Inscription recording the
donation of the manuscript to
Norwich Cathedral Priory by
Robert of Ormesby. Oxford,
Bodleian Library MS. Douce 366,
fol. 1v.

and the date 1654 on the front flyleaf perhaps reveal the name of a seventeenth-century owner.

Once the Psalter emerged into the daylight of the nineteenth century, its supreme quality was recognized immediately by bibliophiles. Engravings of parts of the borders appeared in Henry Shaw's 1833 landmark publication *Illuminated Ornaments Selected from Manuscripts and Early Printed Books from the Sixth to the Seventeenth Centuries*.[3] Gustav Waagen, director of the Berlin Gemäldegalerie, stopped at the Bodleian on his 'Grand Tour' of British art collections in the early nineteenth century and was deeply impressed by the manuscript, writing that it was 'of great importance for the history of painting in England'.[4] By the 1880s the Psalter was displayed in a glass case in the Douce Museum on the first floor of the Schools quadrangle of the Bodleian, along with a ninth-century psalter written in gold and silver on purple-stained parchment (MS. Douce 59), the Douce Apocalypse (MS. Douce 180) and the Hours of Englebert of Nassau (MS. Douce 219–20), august company indeed.[5] In 1905 Bodleian Librarian E.W.B. Nicholson described it as 'the finest MS. executed in England which is in the Bodleian',[6] and in 1907 Sir Sydney Cockerell included it in the East Anglian school in his monograph on the Gorleston Psalter.[7] In 1926 it was the subject of a Roxburghe Club volume in which Cockerell described the manuscript's codicology, texts and decoration in detail.[8] Since then it has been repeatedly cited by art historians as one of the canonical works of English manuscript painting.[9]

Medieval owners

The Ormesby Psalter is one of a handful of medieval manuscripts which appear to offer relatively straightforward evidence of their original provenance. In addition to the prominent inscription recording the donation of the book to Norwich Cathedral Priory on fol. 1v, there are depictions of a monk (presumably Robert himself) and a bishop below the great *Beatus* B on fol. 9v (PLATE I). From the surviving Norwich documents, it seems likely that Robert was subprior of the cathedral in the 1330s (see below). Although the quality of his gift is exceptional, it was not unusual for a monk to buy books which later passed

2 The binding of the Ormesby Psalter with the chemise closed.

4 THE ORMESBY PSALTER

to his monastery. Often this was in the form of a bequest, although the wording of the Ormesby Psalter's inscription suggests that it was presented to Norwich during Robert's lifetime.

Robert, however, was neither the first nor the last owner to wish to leave a tangible record of his association with the manuscript which bears his name. Inside the lower bowl of the *Beatus* B kneel two small donor figures, a man and a woman. They wear heraldic robes displaying the arms of the Foliots (*gules* a bend *argent*) and Bardolfs (*azure* three cinqfoils *or*), two prominent East Anglian landowning families. These arms can be found in a number of other places in the manuscript, along with a wide variety of coats of arms in the line fillers which seemingly constitute a roll-call of the East Anglian nobility of the early fourteenth century. The fore-edges of the book are also painted with heraldic decoration, including the arms of England in the quartering introduced in 1340 (quarterly, 1 and 4, *gules* three leopards passant *or*; 2 and 3, *azure, semé* of fleurs-de-lys *or*), the See of Norwich (*azure* three mitres *or*), the Cathedral Priory (*argent* a cross *sable*) and the Earls of Suffolk (*sable* a cross engrailed *or*). The precise significance of all this heraldry remains elusive and will be discussed in more detail below.

The book as a book

The Ormesby Psalter is an extremely imposing volume. Made up of 213 parchment folios measuring approximately 39.4 × 27.9 cm, it is comparable in size to the largest luxury psalters. It is also in remarkable condition. No pages have been lost or initials cut out, and the manuscript retains its medieval binding of heavy oak boards covered with a tawed skin chemise which wraps around the book like a soft dust jacket (FIGURE 2). Even the painting on the fore-edges, once a widespread feature of medieval manuscripts but largely lost to the vagaries of time and rebinding, remains clearly visible, albeit somewhat faded.

As its name suggests, the book contains the Psalms and Canticles in Latin (fols 10r–205v), preceded by a Calendar and Paschal Table (fols 2r–8v), and followed by two Litanies, each with prayers and petitions (fols 206r–209r and 209v–213r). Of these, the Calendar and second Litany do not form part of the

6   THE ORMESBY PSALTER

original manuscript, but were added when the book was adapted for use at Norwich.

The Psalter's pages boast an astonishing wealth of illumination. The text of the Psalms is preceded by a full-page frontispiece showing an elaborate Tree of Jesse (PLATE 1). Large historiated initials at Psalms 1, 26, 38, 51, 52, 68, 80, 97, 101 and 109 mark the traditional English tenfold division of the Psalms (PLATES 2–11). The opening words of the ordinary psalms and collects have two-line initials, some historiated, some containing foliage or fantastic beasts, picked out in burnished gold and rich colours. Single-line initials in burnished gold on pink and blue grounds mark each verse of the psalms. This hierarchical system, with the largest initials marking the most important places in the text, acted as a navigational tool in an era prior to page or psalm numbering: painting in books was functional as well as fun. Even the blank spaces at the end of each line are filled with ornamental line fillers. The punched and patterned burnished gold would have shone and flickered in the candlelight of a medieval church.

The chief delight and glory of the manuscript are its borders, however. Intertwining tendrils set against cusped panels of pink, blue and gold spring from the initial finials. These wrap around the text and explode in a range of flowers, fruit and foliage, interspersed with geometric patterns and knotwork. Many are inhabited by a vibrant and outlandish crew of monsters and men, beasts, birds and insects, in every probable and improbable combination. Fantastic and incredible imagery proliferates, with cripples and musicians, mermaids and centaurs, lovers and warriors juxtaposed with scenes from everyday life, from courtly myth and chivalric legend, from folk tales, fables and riddles. Running through all are a kind of earthy humour and a satirical view of life, embodied in the 'world upside-down', where animal and human roles are reversed. A knight is terrified by a giant snail, a monkey hunter swings a lure for an owl, hares armed with swords attack a hound, and a fox-pilgrim preaches to a hare. These marvellous margins have charmed viewers from the first – Waagen described the marginalia as 'of spirited invention, and often of delightful humour, with an uncommon feeling for grace' – and have been

INTRODUCTION 7

reproduced countless times on everything from postcards to key rings.

Psalters attracted such lavish illumination because of their unequalled importance in medieval worship. The Old Testament Book of Psalms was the prayer book of the Christian Church from the time of St Augustine, and the liturgy of the Middle Ages consisted largely of the public singing of the psalms. A monk would recite all 150 psalms each week throughout the year, and psalters were kept at altars in cathedrals and churches, and owned and cherished by individual monks and clergy. Before the rise of the Book of Hours, the psalter was also the primary text for lay devotion, and very large and lavish psalters were commissioned by wealthy aristocrats as well as ecclesiastics. Though undoubtedly objects of conspicuous consumption, these were more than just glamorous coffee-table books, and were probably intended for use in private or chantry chapels and perhaps for personal devotional reading.

The puzzle

Not only an object of great beauty in itself, the Ormesby Psalter is of immense art-historical importance. Like many medieval manuscripts, it contains painting in more than one style and was clearly executed by a number of different artists. Scholars agree that it was written and illuminated in a series of campaigns or distinct phases involving successive patrons and groups of artists, from the late thirteenth to the middle of the fourteenth century, so that its pages show a 'panorama of stylistic development' over almost three-quarters of a century.[10] Art historians have argued for over a century as to the precise dating and composition of these campaigns and the nature, relationships and location of the workshop/s responsible.

Artistic collaboration in manuscripts could take different forms. Sometimes the involvement of a number of illuminators was planned from the start, and work was parcelled out by distributing the unbound quires – folded groups of parchment leaves – to different workshops so that they could be worked on simultaneously. In others, it was a matter of necessity rather than choice, as work was interrupted for various reasons, or a book was abandoned incomplete if a patron lost interest, or died.

This sometimes resulted in major changes of plan as text and/ or images were adapted to suit the needs of a new patron. In the case of the Ormesby Psalter, these scenarios came together to produce a particularly intriguing tangle. In its final state the Psalter is the work of four or five scribes, three main illuminators and numerous lesser artists. Work was interrupted at least twice, resulting in major changes of plan, and on certain folios the illumination was left unfinished, revealing the underdrawing and various stages of painting and gilding.

Even the magnificent medieval binding is not as simple as it seems. Binding was the final stage in a book's production, and the manuscript must have been bound for it to be used in the choir at Norwich according to the terms of Robert of Ormesby's donation. Assuming the book to have been bound by Robert, scholars have struggled to account for the presence of the Ufford arms on the fore-edges. It has not been fully appreciated, however, that although the current binding is medieval, it is not the manuscript's first. The evidence is not straightforward, but wormholes created by woodworm from the binding burrowing into fols 208–211, but not the final quire, show that what is now the penultimate quire of the manuscript was once its last. Unused sewing holes in the spine folds of some of the quires, the surprising lack of end bands or channels for them, and the two sets of channels for sewing bands visible on the inner back cover also suggest two distinct phases of binding.

This matters to art historians because the Ormesby Psalter sits at the heart of the so-called East Anglian School, an umbrella term for a group of large, luxury manuscripts, many of which have connections with Norwich Cathedral or diocese, or with Norfolk churches and patrons. The most important of these are the Gorleston Psalter, the Stowe Breviary, the Macclesfield Psalter, the St Omer Psalter and the Douai Psalter.[11] Only the Stowe Breviary and the Douai Psalter can be securely dated from the presence of a set of historical notes ending in 1322, but the group are generally arranged in a chronological sequence based on evolving style, beginning in the 1310s with the Gorleston Psalter and culminating in the St Omer Psalter, generally dated to the 1330s–40s. Art historians have identified a number of scribes and illuminators whose work appears in more than one of these manuscripts, and it has been argued that they represent the evolving output of a single workshop over a number of decades.

Because of the intermittent nature of its production, unravelling the Ormesby Psalter's complexities has sometimes been seen as providing a key to the nature and stylistic development of the East Anglian workshop/s. It is not an easy key to use, however, and Cockerell himself admitted that 'after the closest examination the book has revealed but half its secrets'.[12] The Psalter's main decorated pages stand slightly apart from the stylistic tradition exemplified by the Gorleston Psalter group (FIGURE 3), and it has been suggested that it represents the output of a different workshop. Its relationship with the East Anglian group is more complex than that, however, and a full discussion of it lies outside the scope of the present study. As a first step, the basic who, when, where and why of the various phases of the Psalter's production need to be more clearly established.

Understanding when, where and for whom the Psalter was made is of greater importance than simply elucidating the production processes of English provincial painting. The first half of the fourteenth century saw the beginnings of the fundamental stylistic shift away from the flat, linear forms of early Gothic to a new and more sophisticated understanding of pictorial space and of painterly modelling. Because of the almost total destruction of English medieval wall and panel painting since the Reformation, virtually all our understanding of the development of English painting of this period comes from manuscript illumination. This transformation, which is particularly evident in manuscripts of the East Anglian School and in the pages of the Ormesby Psalter itself, is generally understood as a result of contacts with artistic currents from the Continent, from Paris and northern France in the late thirteenth and early fourteenth centuries, from Italy in the 1320s and 1330s, and from Flanders in the 1340s.[13]

The story I tell in this book represents my current understanding of the making of the Ormesby Psalter, based on a combination of close stylistic and codicological examination of the Psalter itself, an analysis of textual, iconographic and

3 *Beatus* initial with Jesse Tree, Psalm 1, from the Gorleston Psalter, *c.* 1310–20. London, British Library Additional MS. 49622, fol. 8r.

uniuersa terra·
Quoniam eleuata est magnificentia
tua·: super celos·
Ex ore infantium ⁊ lactentium perfecisti
laudem propter inimicos tuos: ut
destruas inimicum ⁊ ultorem·
Quoniam uidebo celos tuos opera di
gitorum tuorum: lunam ⁊ stellas q̄
tu fundasti·
Quid e homo quod memor es eius: aut
filius hominis quoniam uisitas eū
Minuisti eum paulominus ab angelis
gloria ⁊ honore coronasti eum: ⁊ constitu
isti eum super opa manuum tuarū
Omnia subiecisti sub pedibz eius: oues
⁊ boues uniuersas insup ⁊ pecora campi
Uolucres celi ⁊ pisces maris: qui peram
bulant semitas maris·

heraldic evidence, and comparisons with related manuscripts and works in other media. While not attempting to provide definitive solutions to all the problems raised by the book's complex production, I will argue that the manuscript is in some ways less puzzling than has previously been realized. It is important to remember that illuminated manuscripts were not conjured out of the thin air of the Middle Ages but were commissioned and paid for by real people in some actual place at some definable time. What has been identified by art historians as changes in plan can be associated with and sometimes accounted for by events in the life of the commissioner, whom, it should be borne in mind, was not always the same as the intended user. I will argue that much of the decoration of the Ormesby Psalter can be associated with a single patron, and that some of its unusual codicological and stylistic features can be explained and dated by the story of that patron and his immediate circle.

Much of the material in this book is derived from direct examination of manuscripts, from medieval documentary sources and from the work of previous scholars, and it would be possible to footnote almost every sentence. In order not to try the patience of the reader, however, I have kept footnoting to a minimum. Those looking for a more in-depth codicological or stylistic analysis can refer to my unpublished Ph.D. thesis, to my forthcoming article on the East Anglian group, or to previous studies of the manuscript listed in the suggested reading.

Making the Ormesby Psalter

Every medieval manuscript represents a triumph of planning and organization. This is particularly so with deluxe manuscripts where, although the text could be copied from an exemplar, the layout and design are unique to that book. The finished product is the outcome of a series of decisions as to size, quality of materials and extent and nature of decoration, decisions which would have been made by the 'designer', whether that was the scribe, stationer or artist, in response to the requirements of the patron. These decisions were largely dependent on the depth of the patron's pockets and could vary considerably from one patron to the next within a single book.

4 Gothic liturgical hand and penwork line fillers in the Ormesby Psalter, late-thirteenth-century campaign. Oxford, Bodleian Library MS. Douce 366, fol. 16v.

INTRODUCTION   13

Et folium eius non defluet: et omnia quecumque faciet prosperabuntur. Non sic impii non sic: sed tamquam pulvis quem proicit ventus a facie terre.

Ideo non resurgunt impii in iudicio: neque peccatores in consilio iustorum. Quoniam novit dominus viam iustorum: et iter impiorum peribit.

Efficenos domine tamquam fructuosissimum lignum ante conspectum tuum ut tuis umbris irrigari mereamur tibi suavium fructuum ubertate placere. Per.

Quare fremuerunt gentes: et populi meditati sunt inania. Asteterunt reges terre et principes convenerunt in unum: adversus dominum et

Illuminating a psalter presented a particular challenge to the medieval artist because of the nature of the text. The psalms are a series of poems, without any unifying narrative or theme running through them, and various conventions of psalter illustration had developed over the course of the Middle Ages. As in many East Anglian psalters, the initials at the main liturgical divisions of the Ormesby Psalter hark back to an eclectic iconographic programme developed in the thirteenth century combining both French and English elements. The initials of the minor psalms contain a range of subjects, from images of King David, who was identified in the Middle Ages as the author of the psalms, either in prayer or acting out the words of the text, to Christological scenes and Old Testament stories, and images of daily life.

The late-thirteenth-century campaign

From its inception the Ormesby Psalter was intended to be a highly ostentatious object.

Not only is it a big book, measuring more than 15½ by 10 inches (at this size it was never intended to be easily portable), but it was made from the best materials and produced with the utmost care. The original core of the manuscript (fols 10–211) containing the Psalms, Canticles and the first Litany forms a codicologically coherent unit. The text was written by a single scribe on parchment (carefully prepared sheep or cow skin) of a consistently high quality, thick and heavy and a rich ivory colour, with very few flaws. This is folded into quires of twelve leaves, with the exception of the last, which contains only ten, all that was required for the writing of the text. Each quire is marked with a catchword, a system in which the first word of the following quire was written at the bottom of the last page of the previous one, so that the quires could easily be assembled in the correct order when it came to binding the manuscript.

The pages are ruled in lead point in a single column of eighteen lines with very wide margins left around the edges of the text block. The script is a formal Gothic liturgical hand with the downstrokes of the letters squared off horizontally at their bottoms (FIGURE 4). This type of script is known technically as *littera textualis prescissa formata* and was the highest and

5 Q initial with David debating with a group of men. Psalm 2, Ormesby Psalter, late-thirteenth-century campaign. Oxford, Bodleian Library MS. Douce 366, fol. 10v.

INTRODUCTION 15

most expensive grade of Gothic script, being the hardest to produce. The scribe has provided base and headlines, like those in a child's exercise book, an expensive feature designed to ensure that letter size remains constant. The writing is even and careful, but solid and plain, lacking the compressed verticality typical of fourteenth-century hands. Paleographical features suggest a scribe writing in the late thirteenth rather than the early fourteenth century.

The grand intentions indicated by the liberal use of parchment and stately script were borne out by the intended decorative programme. The layout and extent of decoration in a manuscript were largely decided by the scribe/designer well before the painting began. Spaces were left for large initials at the tenfold division of the psalms and for two-line initials at the start of each psalm, canticle and collect, giving almost 350 sites for illumination. Add to these the single-line verse initials in the margins (also a thirteenth- rather than fourteenth-century feature), spaces for initials in the litany and petitions, the blank spaces at the end of each verse of the psalms, and possible illumination in the original Calendar, and the extensive nature of the planned programme becomes clear.

Work on the decoration could be started once the writing of the text was complete. The illumination of this first campaign has been described as 'late thirteenth-century English book-painting at its peak'.[14] The minor initials and line fillers of Section 1 (fols 10r–21v) and some of the verse initials and line fillers in Sections 2 and 3 (fols 22r–45v) were executed by a single workshop and possibly a single artist. The painting in this portion of the book is of exquisite quality, crisp and clear, and executed in brilliant jewel-like colours (FIGURE 5). Alternating pink and blue initials framed in burnished gold are inhabited by small, sturdy figures, often three-quarter length, set against punched or incised gold grounds.

Charming and inventive grotesques inhabit the line fillers or perch on spirals in the margins. A stilt-legged bird with a hare's head shoots an arrow at a white dog (FIGURE 6), a bearded man perches with the body of a bird and the horns of a deer (FIGURE 7), a blue bird places something in the mouth of a dragon with a bishop's head (FIGURE 8). Delicate penwork flourishes, animals,

6 C initial with David kneeling before an altar. Psalm 4, Ormesby Psalter, late-thirteenth-century campaign. Oxford, Bodleian Library MS. Douce 366, fol. 12r.

Uoce mea ad dominum clamaui: et ex
audiuit me de monte sancto suo.
Ego dormiui et soporatus sum: et ex
rexi quia dominus suscepit me.
Non timebo milia populi circumdan
tis me: exurge domine saluum me
fac deus meus.
Quoniam tu percussisti omnes aduer
santes michi sine causa: dentes pecca
torum contriuisti.
Domini est salus: et super populum
tuum benedictio tua.
Effunde domine benedictionem
tuam super populum tuum.
ut tua resurrectione muniti, non timea
mus aduersantium uitiorum milibus
circumdari. Per
cum inuocarem exaudiuit me

7 S initial, Psalm 8, Ormesby Psalter, late-thirteenth-century campaign. Oxford, Bodleian Library MS. Douce 366, fol. 16r.

fish and grotesques occupy the line fillers. The decoration of this early phase bears little resemblance to the somewhat provincial style of Norwich painting seen in a glass roundel of *c.* 1250 now in Saxlingham Nethergate, in the Carrow Psalter and a psalter in Madrid of *c.* 1250–60, and in the angels on the arch of the Ante-Reliquary Chapel in the Cathedral, which possibly date to the 1260s or 1270s.[15] It developed out of that of the mid-thirteenth-century Bible of Richard of Felmingham, which was given to Norwich towards the end of the century (FIGURE 9),[16] and has been compared with a Cambridge charter of the 1290s.[17] It also bears comparison with broader English, northern French and Flemish trends of the late thirteenth century (FIGURE 10), and should perhaps be dated to the last two decades of the century.

18 THE ORMESBY PSALTER

8 I initial with the Ascension. Psalm 10, Ormesby Psalter, late-thirteenth-century campaign. Oxford, Bodleian Library MS. Douce 366, fol. 20r.

9 D initial showing Solomon enthroned above conquered kings, in the Bible of Richard of Felmingham, East Anglia, mid-thirteenth century. Oxford, Bodleian Library MS. Auct. D.4.8, fol. 366v.

At this early stage, the Ormesby Psalter was intended to have a historiated initial – that is, an initial containing an identifiable scene or figures – for each psalm. This level of illustration was extremely unusual, as most illuminated psalters have historiated initials only at the major divisions. If this ambitious programme had been completed it would have constituted one of the richest cycles of psalter illustration produced in medieval England. Most of those initials that were completed contain a straightforward illustration of the adjoining text. Many show David kneeling in prayer before a bust of Christ or acting out the words of the psalm. At Psalm 5 he points to his mouth in response to the first verse of the psalm, *Verba mea auribus percipe domine…* (Give ear O

10 *Beatus* page from the Blackburn Psalter, Oxford(?), c. 1260–80. Blackburn Museum and Art Gallery MS. Hart 21001, fol. 13r.

spiritualem leticiam

spe futurorum munc[rum]

Verba mea auribus

[perci]pe d[omi]ne: intellige cla[morem]

Intende oracionis mee[e]

[de]us meus:

Quoniam ad te orabo d[omine]

[ex]audies uocem mea[m]

Mane astabo tibi 7 uideb[o]

[quoniam non] deus uolens iniquitat[em]

Neq[ue] habitabit iuxta te [malignus]

Lord to my words...) (FIGURE 11). Other figures also reflect the wording of the adjacent verses. At Psalm 8 a bearded man holds up a disc representing the world referred to in verse 1: *Domine dominus noster, quam admirabile est nomen tuum in universa terra* (O Lord, our Lord, how admirable is thy name in the whole earth) (FIGURE 12).

Some initials reflect the medieval understanding of the psalms as prefiguring the Life of Christ. This subject matter suggests an educated and theologically sophisticated audience, with a knowledge of medieval commentaries on the psalms. At Psalm 9 Christ is enthroned at the Last Judgement. Verses 8 and 9 of the psalm refer to God's role as judge, and both Peter Lombard's *Great Gloss* and the *Glossa ordinaria* – the two most important twelfth-century commentaries on the psalms – propose the Last Judgement as the subject of the whole psalm. At Psalm 3, knowledge not only of the commentary but also of the psalm's *titulus* or title – not present in the Ormesby text – would have been needed. The title states that the psalm was composed during David's flight from his son, Absalom, but the initial

11 V initial with David pointing to his mouth. Psalm 5, Ormesby Psalter, late-thirteenth-century campaign. Oxford, Bodleian Library MS. Douce 366, fol. 13r.

12 D initial with a man holding a globe of the world. Psalm 8, Ormesby Psalter, late-thirteenth-century campaign. Oxford, Bodleian Library MS. Douce 366, fol. 16r.

INTRODUCTION   23

shows Christ stepping from the tomb (FIGURE 13). According to both Peter Lombard and the *Glossa ordinaria* David and Absalom were to be understood as prefigurations of Christ and Judas, and the true subject of the psalm was the mystery of the Passion and Resurrection. Only a viewer well acquainted with the psalms and their scholastic interpretation would have appreciated the significance of this initial.

We do not know where or for whom the manuscript was being produced during this first campaign, except presumably it was not for use in Norwich. There is no heraldry in the decoration, the original Calendar does not survive and the original Litany is disappointingly colourless. The only English saints included are Dunstan, Thomas and Edmund, all widely found, and there are no double invocations that might indicate the patron saint of a particular cathedral or abbey.

The text itself, however, offers hints as to the context in which the manuscript was intended to be used, if not the precise location. Each psalm is followed by a collect, a short prayer summarizing the spiritual content of the psalm. By the thirteenth century these prayers had long since ceased to form part of the liturgy but were sometimes retained in the private recitation of the psalter, mainly in a monastic context.[18] Even here they were far from common and seem to have been the mark of a 'special' book. The same series as in the Ormesby Psalter is found in the Tickhill Psalter, written and perhaps

13 D initial with the Resurrection. Psalm 3, Ormesby Psalter, late-thirteenth-century campaign. Oxford, Bodleian Library MS. Douce 366, fol. 11v.

24   THE ORMESBY PSALTER

illuminated by John Tickhill, prior of Workshop Priory, Nottinghamshire, probably for his own use.[19] The Ormesby Psalter was perhaps likewise intended for the private reading of a senior member of a religious house. The first Litany includes a request for protection for founders and benefactors more appropriate for a book destined for use in a religious community than in a private milieu.

Whoever this individual was, he cannot have had much opportunity to enjoy his psalter. Work on the manuscript was suspended with only the minor initials and line fillers in Section 1 and the verse initials and designs for some of the line fillers in Sections 2 and 3 complete. Once halted, work on the Psalter was not resumed for some time.

The 1310s campaign: the Bardolfs, the Foliots and the Earl of Surrey

The Ormesby Psalter was both fortunate and unfortunate in its next patrons. Between 1310 and 1320 work on the manuscript was resumed to meet the needs of two prominent East Anglian families, the Foliots and the Bardolfs, whose arms can be found scattered in initials, borders and line fillers through its pages.

14 Foliot and Bardolf donor figures on the Ormesby Psalter, 1310s campaign. Oxford, Bodleian Library MS. Douce 366, fol. 9v.

am tuam famulis tuis supplicib3: 7 fac
nos in tua ueritate deuotos. ut actib3 n̄ris
⁊ innocentia restitutis. liberari mereamur
ab impiis. per

ominus illuminatio
mea et salus mea: quē
timebo

D̄s, ptector uite mee:
a quo trepidabo

Dum appropiant super me nocentes: ut e
dant carnes meas.

Qui tribulant me inimici mei: ipsi infir
mati sunt ⁊ ceciderunt.

Si consistant aduersum me castra: non ti
mebit cor meum.

Si exurgat aduersum me prelium: in hoc
ego sperabo.

Unam petii a domino hanc requiram: ut i

In addition to the two figures in heraldic robes on the *Beatus* frontispiece (FIGURE 14), at Psalm 26 a knight standing next to the initial bears on his shield and tunic the charge *gules* a bend *or*, a variant on the Foliot arms (FIGURE 15).[20] The shield and epaulettes of the knight battling the dragon in the lower border of Psalm 97 are decorated with the Foliot arms but with the bend left white, a common alternative to silver (FIGURE 16). Bardolf flowers and the Foliot diagonal stripe are juxtaposed in the line fillers of fol. 154r (FIGURE 17), and were sketched in the line fillers of Sections 14 and 17, although these were overpainted as part of a later campaign. There are a variety of other coats of arms in the line fillers representing a coterie of families associated with the Bardolfs and Foliots, or with John de Warenne (d. 1347), Earl of Surrey and Sussex, feudal overlord of both families.

15 (*opposite*) D initial with knight in upright bearing variant on Foliot arms, and adjoining lines with Warenne arms in line filler. Psalm 26, Ormesby Psalter, 1310s campaign. Oxford, Bodleian Library MS. Douce 366, fol. 38r.

16 Lower border with Foliot knight fighting a dragon. Psalm 97, Ormesby Psalter, 1310s campaign. Oxford, Bodleian Library MS. Douce 366, fol. 128r.

INTRODUCTION 27

inimicos meos.

Bonum est confidere in domino: quam 2
fidere in homine.

Bonum est sperare in domino: quam :
sperare in principibus.

Omnes gentes circuierunt me: 7 in nomie
domini quia ultus sum in eos.

Circundantes circundederunt me: 7 in nomi
ne domini quia ultus sum in eos.

Circumdederunt me sicut apes 7 exarserut
sicut ignis in spinis: 7 in nomine dni
quia ultus sum in eos.

Impulsus euersus sum ut caderem: 7 do
minus suscepit me.

Fortitudo mea 7 laus mea dominus: 7 fac
tus e michi in salutem.

Vox exultationis et salutis: in taberna
culis iustorum.

There seems to have been some urgency in this campaign. Taking advantage of the inherent flexibility of medieval manuscripts, the unbound and partially decorated quires were split between a number of different illuminators so that they could be worked on simultaneously. Two highly skilful and innovative artists executed the large initials and borders at the main liturgical divisions. The minor decoration was then parcelled out quire by quire.[21] In spite of this apparent haste, the manuscript was once more abandoned unfinished, with the decoration on some pages only partially complete. What could account for such urgency followed by a sudden loss of interest?

Close investigation of the Foliot and Warenne families' circumstances can both narrow the dating range for this second campaign and account for the Psalter's sudden abandonment. The small male figure on the *Beatus* frontispiece has generally been identified as Richard Foliot the younger, who died a minor before 29 May 1325, his death providing a *terminus ante quem* for work on this phase of the manuscript. Given the ages of his sisters and the dates of his parents' marriage, he was probably born in 1311. Young Richard's father, however, was killed on military service in Scotland before 5 March 1316, possibly at Bannockburn in 1314. At this point, according to feudal law, the young Richard Foliot became the ward of John de Warenne. The Foliot wardship formed part of a series of punishing settlements drawn up from November 1318 to Easter 1319 between Warenne and his archenemy Thomas, Earl of Lancaster, in which Warenne released his claim to it to Lancaster, along with his lands in Yorkshire, North Wales and Norfolk. I will argue below that the second campaign of work on the Psalter was commissioned by Warenne for his ward to commemorate the latter's betrothal and can thus be dated to between Warenne's obtaining the Foliot guardianship in *c.* 1314–16 and losing it in 1318–19.

The Jesse Master

Medieval artists were anonymous, so we do not know the identities of the two principal painters of this phase of the decoration. Sections 1, 2 and 3 (fols 10r–45v), which had been partially decorated in the thirteenth century, were given to a talented illuminator whom I have dubbed the Jesse Master after the splendid

17 Foliot and Bardolf arms in line fillers, Ormesby Psalter, 1310s campaign. Oxford, Bodleian Library MS. Douce 366, fol. 154r.

INTRODUCTION 29

abit in consilio impiorum ⁊ in uia
peccatorum non stetit: ⁊ in cathe-
dra pestilentie non sedit
Set in lege domini uoluntas ei: ⁊ i[n]
lege eius meditabitur die ac nocte
Et erit tamquam lignum qd pla[n]-
tatum e secus decursus aquaru: qd
fructum suu dabit in tempore suo

frontispiece which now faces Psalm 1 (PLATE 1 and FIGURE 18). He and his workshop also executed the large initial and border for Psalm 26 (PLATE 3 and FIGURE 15) and the minor initials and remaining line fillers in Sections 2 and 3 (fols 22r–45v).

The decoration of Psalm 1 offers an excellent example of the problems encountered in unravelling the various stages of work on this manuscript. As the opening for the Psalter proper, the initial B of *Beatus* was one of the main sites for illumination in medieval psalters. Most unusually, however, the Ormesby Psalter has two *Beatus* initials facing each other across a single opening (FIGURE 18). On fol. 9v the great B is filled and surrounded by an extensive Tree of Jesse, while on the opposite page, fol. 10r, an aged King David sits on a throne playing a harp. Both the Jesse Tree and David as a musician were conventional illustrations for Psalm 1: David as the Psalms' author, and the Jesse Tree showing the descent of Christ from Jesse through David.

This double *Beatus* was not planned from the start, however, but is the result of a succession of changes of plan during the course of the production of the manuscript. The Jesse Tree is painted on a single leaf, which has been tipped into the manuscript the wrong way round, so that its intended recto is now its verso. Although it has sometimes been argued that this leaf has migrated from another manuscript, textual and codicological evidence show that it was made as a replacement for the first leaf of the original text. Not only is the psalm followed by its collect, a highly unusual textual feature paralleled in the main body of the Psalter, but the text ends at exactly the same place on both fols 9r and 10v, with the words *adversus dominum et*. This planned substitution was never carried out, however, and the leaf was bound into the manuscript in a reversed position, facing the page it was supposed to replace.

The frontispiece was clearly of great importance to the patrons of this second campaign. Aside from the care with which it was painted and gilded, and the inclusion of the donor figures prominently asserting their ownership of the manuscript, the financial implications of a decision to create a new leaf must have required the patron's direct involvement. What did they want that could not be fitted into the considerable space left around the text on the original first leaf?

18   (*previous spread*) The double *Beatus* opening in the Ormesby Psalter, 1310s and 1330s campaigns. Oxford, Bodleian Library MS. Douce 366, fols 9v and 10r.

The Ormesby *Beatus* Jesse Tree is exceptional in terms of both scale and layout, in comparison with those found in contemporary manuscripts. In general Jesse Trees in medieval psalters were contained inside the B initial, sometimes with subsidiary figures in rectilinear borders running around the text block. Here, however, both initial and text are subsumed among the writhing strands of foliage and jostling figures. Space was left for only four lines of script below the B, as compared to eight on the facing page, and the central stem of the Tree runs directly up through the centre of the text block, considerably reducing the legibility of the text.

The painting itself is of an extremely high quality. Monumental figures of kings and prophets are contained in compartments formed by the criss-crossing branches of the Tree. No two are alike, and their dancing poses, lively expressions and gesticulating hands make it seem as if they are engaged in animated conversation across the page. The diversity of position and expression is paralleled by the richness and variety of dress: tunics and cloaks of differing colours, cloaks with contrasting linings, patterned sleeves and hems, hats in all shapes and sizes. Draperies fall in broad swathes, and are picked out in an unusual palette of soft pink, slate grey, deep blue, mustard yellow and brown. The artist has even achieved the effect of a translucent veil on the female donor figure, and of a broad self-stripe on Jesse's underblanket.

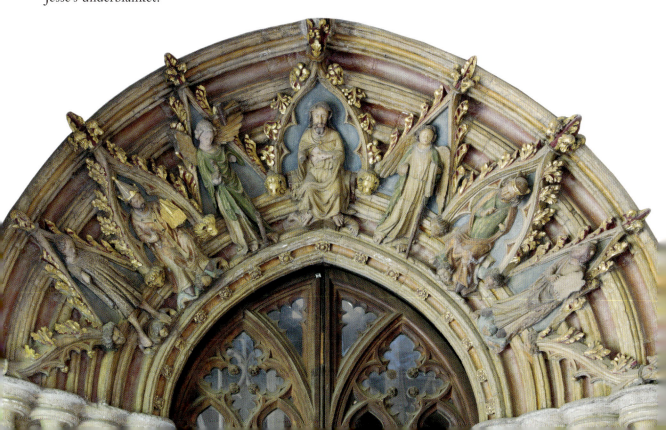

19 Christ flanked by angels and saints. Norwich Cathedral Cloister, Prior's Door, *c.* 1300–1320.

20 Stained-glass figures of prophets from a Jesse window, St Peter's, Lowick, Northamptonshire, c. 1317.

The closest parallels to the Jesse Master's style can be found not in manuscript painting but in sculpture and stained glass of the early decades of the fourteenth century. The sculpted decoration of Norwich Cathedral Cloister was completed in a series of campaigns from the late thirteenth century onwards.[22] The elongated proportions of the kings and prophets recall the figures over the Prior's Door in the north-east corner of the cloister (FIGURE 19), while the broad soft folds of the Jesse Master's drapery echo both the Door sculptures and the bosses of Christ's Passion in the first five bays of the east walk of the Cloister. The balancing of the prophet figures pose against pose also recalls the standing saints painted on the wall of the Norwich Ante-Reliquary Chapel.[23]

The Ormesby prophets and kings have also been compared with the surviving figures of a stained-glass Jesse Tree from Lowick in Northamptonshire, perhaps datable to c. 1317 (FIGURE 20).[24] The structure of the Ormesby Tree, with its symmetrical kings and prophets in medallions forming inner and outer lancets, is strongly reminiscent of the large multi-light Jesse windows which became popular in the fourteenth century.

Although none of the Ormesby figures is precisely paralleled in the Lowick glass, the Foliots had a historical connection with the area immediately around Lowick,[25] and Jesse Trees were once found in a number of churches in the area. Could the Ormesby frontispiece have been inspired by such a window, or perhaps by a *vidimus* for one?[26]

Whatever the sources of the Ormesby Jesse Tree design, it rapidly became well known to East Anglian illuminators. It is one of several elements of the Ormesby Psalter's decorative scheme echoed in the Macclesfield Psalter of the 1320s or early 1330s (FIGURE 21), and a version of it also appears in a small psalter perhaps made for Edward III *c.* 1325–35.[27]

The Jesse Master and his workshop also executed the initial and border at Psalm 26 and the minor initials in Sections 2 and 3. The Psalm 26 page combines a virtuosic painting of grotesques and an intense observation of the natural world with

21 *Beatus* page with Tree of Jesse, Psalm 1, from the Macclesfield Psalter, *c.* 1325–30. Cambridge, Fitzwilliam Museum MS. 1–2005, fol. 9r.

22 C initial with bellows player in margin. Collect for Psalm 15, Ormesby Psalter, 1310s campaign. Oxford, Bodleian Library MS. Douce 366, fol. 24r.

startling shifts of scale. In the minor initials the crispness of the late-thirteenth-century work has been replaced by a freer and more opulent manner characteristic of the 1310s and 1320s, with large figures in borders and margins beside the initials (FIGURE 22). Although the quality of the painting in this section is somewhat uneven, occasional figures leap out as if spotlit, and reveal the hand of the Master. At Psalm 15, a beautifully painted snail-trumpeter, his horn forming the initial I of the collect, announces the Day of Doom in the psalm initial, when the dead rise from their graves to be judged by the risen Christ (FIGURE 23). The anxious gaze of the bearded layman in the collect to

Psalm 25 is not only vividly expressive of the emotional appeal of the text, but is so individual as to suggest that it might have been intended to represent a particular person (FIGURE 24). The man wears a slender circlet, and the face bears a striking resemblance to the head of the tomb sculpture of Edward II at Tewkesbury Abbey, a king who might well have needed to call on God for relief from his enemies.

23 C initial with Last Judgement. Psalm 15, Ormesby Psalter, 1310s campaign. Oxford, Bodleian Library MS. Douce 366, fol. 23v.

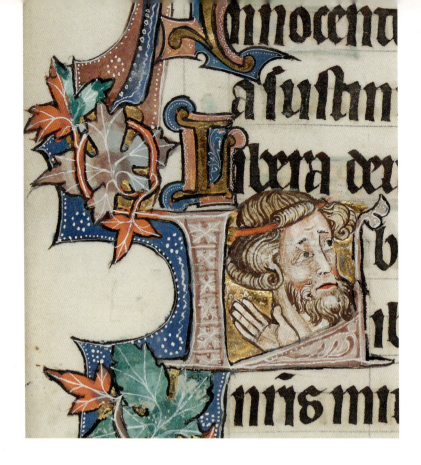

The verse initials and some of the line fillers of Sections 2 and 3 had been executed as part of the thirteenth-century campaign. The Jesse Master retained those with penwork flourishing, but painted over those showing animals and zoomorphs and added a number of new ones containing coats of arms (FIGURE 25). Of these by far the most numerous is the blue and gold check of the Earls of Warenne. At Psalm 26 the Warenne shield is positioned directly above the word *dominus*, 'Lord', which in medieval Latin could refer to either the Lord God or a temporal, feudal lord (FIGURE 15). Both the Bardolfs and the Foliots held much of their extensive Norfolk landholdings in military tenure from the earls of Warenne, and John de Warenne, the last earl, was particularly closely connected with both families (see below). The abundant heraldic decoration in the line fillers also includes the coats of arms of Newmarch (*gules* five fusils conjoined in a fess *or*), Percy (*azure* five fusils conjoined in a fess *or*), Clare (*argent* three chevrons *gules*) and Cornwall (*argent*, a lion rampant *gules* within a bordure *sable* bezanty) with single examples of those of Balliol (*gules* an escutcheon voided *argent*), Bohun of Midhurst (*azure* a cross *or*), Castile and Leon (quarterly, 1 and 4 *argent* a lion rampant *sable*,

24 L initial with bearded male head. Psalm 25, Ormesby Psalter, 1310s campaign. Oxford, Bodleian Library MS. Douce 366, fol. 37r.

25 (*opposite*) E initial with Jew asperging a temple. Psalm 29, Ormesby Psalter, 1310s campaign. Oxford, Bodleian Library MS. Douce 366, fol. 41r.

38 THE ORMESBY PSALTER

dominus benedicet populo suo in pace.
Dona domine uirtutem populo tuo.
Et efficie nos templum sps sancti
ut tibi corde puro holocaustum accepta
bile preparemur. per.
Exaltabo te domine qm suscepisti
me: nec delectasti inimicos meos
super me.
Dne deus meus clamaui ad te: 7 sanasti me.
Domine eduxisti ab inferno animam me
am: saluasti me a descendentibz in lacum.
Psallite domino sancti eius: 7 confitemini
memorie sanctitatis eius.
Qm ira in indignatione eius: 7 uita in
uoluntate eius.
Ad uesperum demorabitur fletus: 7 ad ma
tutinum leticia.
Ego autem dixi in habundantia mea: non

Quis est iste rex glorie: ...
...ium ipe est rex glorie.

Stabilitor deus t...
...di plenitudo des...

In innocentia mee: ut p...
...o montem sanctificatio...
...d te domine leua...
...am: deus meus...
...erubescam·

Neq; irrideant me inimi...
...niuersi qui sustinent t...

Confundantur omnes...
...superuacue

...ias tuas domine deme...

2 and 3 *gules* a castle *or*), Fitzalan (*gules* a lion rampant *or*), Varenne (*gules* a cross *or*) and Vaux (chequy *or* and *gules*).

This range of seemingly unconnected coats of arms has sometimes been seen simply as a roll-call of the great and good of early-fourteenth-century England, but a close examination suggests a more coherent programme. The Newmarch, Bohun, Clare, Cornwall and Castile arms allude to family and feudal connections of the Foliots. Margery de Newmarch (d. 1330) was Richard Foliot's grandmother, and his mother, Joan, had formerly been married to James de Bohun of Midhurst (d. before May 1306). The Foliots held various manors in Norfolk and Essex of the Honour of Clare, and the Earl of Gloucester was named as joint guardian of Richard Foliot in a Feudal Aid of 1302.[28] The last Earl of Gloucester, Gilbert de Clare, died at Bannockburn in 1314 and his vast estates passed to his three sisters. De Clare's grandmother was Eleanor of Castile (d. 1290) and his second sister Margaret became Countess of Cornwall when she married Edward II's favourite, Piers Gaveston, in 1307.

Other arms represent the elite Warenne network of aunts, cousins and in-laws. The Percy fusils were borne by John de Warenne's aunt, Eleanor de Percy (d. after 1282), mother of Henry, 1st Baron Percy of Alnwick (d. 1314), and ancestress of the earls of Northumberland. His other aunt, Isabella, was married to John Balliol, King of Scotland (d. 1314), and her son Edward was Warenne's ward up to 1310. Edmund Fitzalan, Earl of Arundel (d. 1326), had been a ward of John's grandfather, and married his sister, Alice, in 1305. Varenne was the French branch of the Warenne family and the name of the village from which they originated. The Vaux arms perhaps allude to Margaret de Nerford, Warenne's long-term mistress and mother of his sons, who was the daughter of Petronilla de Vaux. The Nerford and Bardolf families held neighbouring lands in the Hundred of Holt in Norfolk, and the Vaux and Bardolf arms are juxtaposed in the celebrated Vaux-Bardolf Psalter in Lambeth.[29] A number of other coats in this section are also found in the Vaux-Bardolf Psalter and may well represent wider connections of the Bardolf family. Heraldry in fourteenth-century manuscripts often alludes to now hidden associations between neighbouring families and individuals. The Ormesby Psalter's abundant display of coats of

26 A initial with kneeling bearded man. Psalm 24, Ormesby Psalter, 1310s campaign. Oxford, Bodleian Library MS. Douce 366, fol. 35v.

INTRODUCTION 41

Magnificant salutes regis e

misediam xpo suo dauid:

usq; in seculum·

irmamentum spe

pressure piissime c

ab inimicis nris 7 a laque

assumpta de multitudine

um tribulationum deuotiss

mini tuo cu innocentie p

mus· per·

eli enarrant gloria

manuum eius annuntia

ies diei eructat uerbum· 7

dicat scientiam·

arms serves to establish and reinforce class identity. The Bardolfs and Foliots are presenting themselves as they would like to be seen by their contemporaries: intimately connected with the Warenne Earls and through them with the great and the good of the land.

The initials of Sections 2 and 3 adhere to the thirteenth-century programme of alternating historiated and decorated initials for psalms and collects. Some of the psalm initials show David kneeling in prayer or figures acting out the words of the psalm. At Psalm 24 a bearded layman kneels beneath a battlemented arch and looks up to the right, in response to the opening words of the psalm, *Ad te domine levavi animam meam* (To thee O Lord have I lifted up my soul) (FIGURE 26). His beard and greying locks indicate that he is no longer young, corresponding to the psalmist's appeal to the Lord in verse 7, where he begs him not to remember 'the sins of my youth and my ignorance'. Others have biblical or Christological subjects. The initial at Psalm 18, a hymn of praise, contains the Virgin and Child (FIGURE 27), while at Psalm 19 the Sacrifice of Isaac is depicted, in response to verse 4, *Memor sit omnis sacrificii tui* (May he be mindful of all thy sacrifices) (FIGURE 28). Psalm 21, whose opening words, *Deus deus meus respice in me quare me dereliquisti*, were echoed by

27 (*opposite*) C initial with Virgin and Child. Psalm 18, Ormesby Psalter, 1310s campaign. Oxford, Bodleian Library MS. Douce 366, fol. 29r.

28 E initial with Sacrifice of Isaac. Psalm 19, Ormesby Psalter, 1310s campaign. Oxford, Bodleian Library MS. Douce 366, fol. 30r.

29 (*right*) D initial, Crucifixion. Psalm 21, Ormesby Psalter, 1310s campaign. Oxford, Bodleian Library MS. Douce 366, fol. 32r.

30 (*below*) B initial, youth confessing to a friar. Psalm 31, Ormesby Psalter, 1310s campaign. Oxford, Bodleian Library MS. Douce 366, fol. 44r.

Christ on the Cross, is illustrated with the Crucifixion (FIGURE 29). Others simply respond to the overall theme of the psalm, as at the musical Psalm 32, where a young man plays a viol in the initial, while another dances and plays the pipes in the border.

Occasionally the initials reflect aspects of daily life and hint at layers of meaning beyond the immediate text. At Psalm 31 a friar in the brown habit of a Franciscan hears confession from a young layman (FIGURE 30). This responds not only to verse 5, *Delictum meum cognitum tibi feci* (I have acknowledged my sin to thee), but also to Psalm 31's role as one of the Penitential Psalms,

a group of seven psalms particularly expressive of contrition for sin. The Franciscans had arrived in Norwich in 1226, and by the late thirteenth century were flourishing, commencing work on a grand new church in 1299. John de Warenne had a special interest in the order. He had been married in the Franciscan church in Newgate in 1306, had a Franciscan confessor and was a patron of the Franciscan priories at Gorleston and Grantham. His arms appear in a copy of the writings of the Franciscan theologian Duns Scotus now in Paris.[30]

The Ormesby Master

While Sections 1, 2 and 3 were in the hands of the Jesse Master, the remaining quires were sent to the outstanding artist of the book, the celebrated Ormesby Master. This versatile and witty painter illuminated the remaining liturgical divisions and sketched designs for several further pages in Section 4 (PLATES 4–11 and FIGURE 31). Unlike the Jesse Master, he seems to have been working alone. His pages are consistently of the highest quality, and the prominence of his work suggests that he was responsible for distributing the quires to other illuminators once he had finished the main pages.

His pages exude energy. Initials and borders are inhabited by solid, weighty figures with square-jawed faces, who gesture forcefully at each other or are contorted into dramatic postures. Draperies either cling, revealing the forms of limbs beneath, or fall in smooth, deep folds. At the major divisions vegetation springs from the initial finials and swarms around the text, its stems twisting, turning and tying themselves into complex geometric knots. These tendrils sprout an abundance of foliage, flowers and fruits, both fantastic and naturalistic, including oak, maple and ivy leaves, pea flowers and pods, cornflowers and acorns. The borders bulge and contract, providing a habitat for a cornucopia of probable and improbable beasts, often in hugely contrasted scales. He displays a particular liking for bipeds with canine heads, for creatures either with heads in place of their genitals, or with long tails ending in pointing hands, whose antics add to the sense of disorder. This riotous opulence is given structure by the arrangement of vignettes at both the top and the bottom of the page, many of which mirror or mock the subjects of the initials. Both initials and borders display a pronounced taste for esoteric visual games, as the artist drew on a wide range of contemporary fables, folklore and literature to create intriguing analogies for the sacred histories in the initials.

The Ormesby Master's three-dimensional modelling is especially evident in the nudes, whose ample limbs seem to protrude from the page (FIGURE 32). This feature in particular has been seen by scholars as owing a debt to Italian art of the early fourteenth century. In 1943 Otto Pächt described the Ormesby Master's style as a 'Giottoesque episode in English medieval art' and perceived sources for it in Roman sepulchral sculpture, perhaps transmitted by illuminated Bolognese legal texts.[31] More immediately, however, his distinct aesthetic sensibility owes much to sculpture and illumination produced in the County of Bar, on the north-eastern borders of France, then part of the Holy Roman Empire. His dog-headed monsters, nudes and battling figures vividly recall both the sculptures on the north door of the Cathedral of St Étienne at Metz, and the borders of a magnificent set of liturgical books made for Renaud de Bar, Bishop of Metz (d. 1316).[32] The illumination of these was divided among a group of artists whose origins can be traced to the artistic milieu of Lorraine, the most original of whom shares the Ormesby Master's predilection for contorted figures, startling contrasts of scale and intricate geometric interlace, all arranged in full borders structured by large, secular imagery in the lower margin (FIGURE 33).[33]

Indeed, the similarities are so great that it has been suggested that one of the de Bar artists was an English illuminator working in France.[34] The painterly and sculptural qualities of the Ormesby Master are more developed, however, and it seems equally possible that either the influence or the artists themselves travelled not from England to Metz but in the other direction. Renaud's manuscripts were abandoned unfinished, probably upon his sudden death, allegedly from poisoning, on 4 May 1316. Both manuscripts and their makers were highly mobile at this period and Continental craftsmen were a well-established if minor part of the artistic community in Norwich in the early fourteenth century.[35] There were, moreover, strong family links between the East Anglian and Messin aristocracies in the late

31 Ormesby Master underdrawings from the 1310s campaign overpainted by the Cheap Finisher. Ormesby Psalter, Oxford, Bodleian Library MS. Douce 366, fol. 50r.

maligna loquuntur super me.

Exultent et letentur qui volunt iusticiam meam: et dicant semper magnificetur dominus qui volunt pacem serui eius.

Et lingua mea meditabitur iusticiam tuam: tota die laudem tuam.

Protectio salutisque anime nostre deus propter nos galea salutis et spei et scuto inexpugnabilis munimenta: quesumus ut a te in causis nostre necessitatis adiuti. merantur in te diligentibus leticia et exultatione perfundi. Per.

Dixit iniustus ut delinquat in semet ipso: non est timor dei ante oculos eius.

Quoniam dolose egit in conspectu eius: ut inueniatur iniquitas eius ad odium.

Verba oris eius iniquitas et dolus: noluit intelligere ut bene ageret.

32 Ormesby Psalter, Oxford, Bodleian Library MS. Douce 366, fol. 147v, showing detail of the naked trumpeter and battle between a lion and a bear.

33 Breviary of Renaud de Bar, with *bas-de-page* figures of a young woman playing a rebec, and man and woman with falcon. Verdun, Bibliothèque municipale MS. 107, fol. 12r, before 1316.

thirteenth and early fourteenth centuries. In 1293/4 Eleanor, daughter of Edward I and Eleanor of Castile, had married Henri III, Comte de Bar, brother of Bishop Renaud. Henri and Eleanor's daughter, Joan, became a ward of Edward I on her father's death in 1302, and in 1306 was married to John de Warenne. Although the marriage was notoriously unsuccessful, the de Bar arms occur in a line filler on fol. 60r of the Ormesby Psalter and those of Warenne are found in some of the de Bar manuscripts.[36] Could one speculate that when commissions dried up in Metz one or more of Renaud's illuminators made their way to East Anglia to work for their late patron's brother-in-law? This is a tempting hypothesis, but the extent and nature of the interchanges between English and Continental stained glass, sculpture and manuscript painting needs further investigation.[37]

Whatever his origins, the Ormesby Master was a highly productive and influential artist, producing books for secular and ecclesiastical patrons in and around Norwich. A number of other manuscripts can be attributed to him, including a large psalter for the use of Bromholm Priory at Bacton on the northeast coast of Norfolk (FIGURE 34), a copy of Gregory the Great's

Moralia in Job probably made for Norwich Cathedral Priory, and a picture-book Apocalypse, now in Dublin, whose abbreviated Anglo-Norman French text was perhaps intended for a lay aristocratic audience.[38] The later impact of his style can be seen in a Norwich Book of Hours perhaps of the 1330s, a bestiary in Cambridge and a copy of Martinus Polonus, *Chronicles of the Roman Emperors and Popes*.[39] Versions of his 'tubicinarius' figure also make an appearance in the borders of the Macclesfield Psalter (FIGURE 35).

The impact of his distinctive style was not confined to manuscript painting. A closely related figure style appears on the Thornham Parva Retable, where the soft broad folds of the drapery and elegant gestures of St Edmund vividly recall the king in the border of Psalm 52 (FIGURE 36). This great wooden altar panel, probably commissioned by John de Warenne for the Dominican Priory at Thetford, is securely datable on the basis of tree-ring analysis to after 1317, though it is generally dated by scholars to c. 1330–40.[40] The comic conflicts and

34 D initial with a fool and a man debating from the Bromholm Psalter, Psalm 52, c. 1310–20. Oxford, Bodleian Library MS. Ashmole 1523, fol. 66r.

35 (opposite) Bas-de-page trumpeters in the Macclesfield Psalter, c. 1325–30. Cambridge, Fitzwilliam Museum MS. 1–2005, fol. 39r.

50 THE ORMESBY PSALTER

36 Thornham Parva Retable. St Mary's, Thornham Parva, Suffolk, after 1317.

entwined animals in the roof bosses in the east walk of Norwich Cathedral Cloister, variously dated by scholars to between 1297 and 1314, to before 1329 and to *c.* 1320–30, have frequently been compared with the decoration of the Psalter (FIGURE 37).[41] A similar spirit is evident in the vigorously twisting musicians and dancers and the scatological grotesques in the aisles of St Margaret's at Cley-next-the-Sea, perhaps attributable to the same masons as worked in the Cloister at Norwich (FIGURE 38). Battling monsters and men struggle in tangled foliage in the spandrels of Norwich's St Ethelbert Gate, of after 1316 (FIGURE 39), and in the very worn spandrels of the surviving arch at St Benet's Abbey, Holme, in the Norfolk Broads. A musical centaur at St Peter's Church at Ringland could have trotted off the pages of the manuscript (FIGURE 40).[42]

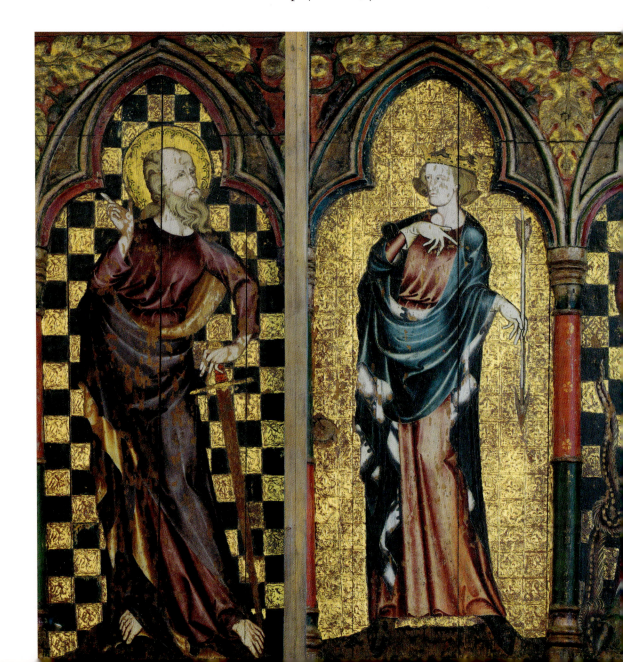

37 (*top*) Norwich Cathedral Cloister, roof boss, *c.* 1310–20.

38 (*left*) Cley-next-the-Sea, St Margaret's, Norfolk, musician, *c.* 1310–20.

Sadly only the initials and borders at the main liturgical divisions of the Psalter were completed by the Ormesby Master himself. His designs for minor initials in Section 4 (fols 45r–57v) were crudely overpainted in a later campaign. Nothing can now be discerned of the psalm initials, but the borders were clearly intended to contain figural decoration: a hand reaches out from beneath the overpainting to grasp a tendril on fol. 48r (FIGURE 41).

Speed was evidently of the essence as in places the Master has truncated his own designs. In the lower border of Psalm 97 the dragon has not only lost two heads to the sword of the knight, but at least one to the pen of the artist: an erased sketch for a seventh head can be discerned

39 (*right*) Norwich Cathedral, St Ethelbert Gate, after 1316.

40 (*above*) St Peter's, Ringland, Norfolk, musical centaur, *c.* 1310–20.

41 (*opposite*) Ormesby Master underdrawings from 1310s campaign overpainted by Cheap Finisher, Psalm 34. Oxford, Bodleian Library MS. Douce 366, fol. 48r.

42 (*overleaf*) D and P initials and borders. Psalms 45 and 46, Ormesby Psalter, 1310s campaign. Oxford, Bodleian Library MS. Douce 366, fols 64v and 65r.

54   THE ORMESBY PSALTER

Angelorum z totius creature dispo
sitor deus. emitte sanctum ange
lum tuum seruituti nostre cuius ambi
tione muniti: mereamur a peccatorum
ipessi liberari. per.

Judica domine nocentes me: expug
na impugnantes me.

Apprehende arma z scutum: z exurge i
adiutorium michi.

Effunde frameam z conclude aduersus
eos qui persequuntur me: dic anime
mee salus tua ego sum.

Confundantur et reuereantur: queren
tes animam meam.

Auertantur retrorsum z confundantur:
cogitantes michi mala.

Fiant tamquam puluis ante faciem uen
ti: z angelus domini coartans eos.

propterea populi confitebuntur tibi in eternum: et in seculum seculi

Xpe domine verbum patris, per quem cuncta creata sunt et creantur: custodi qs ecclesiam varietate gentium aggregatam: ut dum te ex ipsa credulitatis iusticia corde puro diligimus, principatum eterni seculi cum patribz mereamur: salvator mundi, qui cum patre et

Deus nr refugium et virtus: adiutor in tribulationibz que invenerunt nos nimis.

Propterea non timebimus dum turbabitur terra: et transferentur montes in cor maris.

Sonuerunt et turbate sunt aque eor: conturbate sunt montes in fortitudine eius.

Fluminis impetus letificat civitatem dei:

sanctificauit tabernaculum suum al
tissimus.
 eus in medio eius non cōmouebitur:
adiuuabit eam deus mane diluculo.
 onturbate sunt gentes ⁊ inclinata sunt
regna: dedit uocem suam mota ē terra.
 ominus uirtutum nobiscum: suscep
tor noster deus iacob.
 enite ⁊ uidete opera domini: que posuit
prodigia super terram.
 uferens bella usq̇ ad finem terre arcum
conteret ⁊ confringet arma: ⁊ scuta com
buret igni.
 acate ⁊ uidete qm̄ ego sum deus: exalta
bor in gentibȝ ⁊ exaltabor in terra.
 ominus uirtutum nobiscum suscep
tor nr̄ deus iacob.
 erspicuum in eminenti rsfugiū

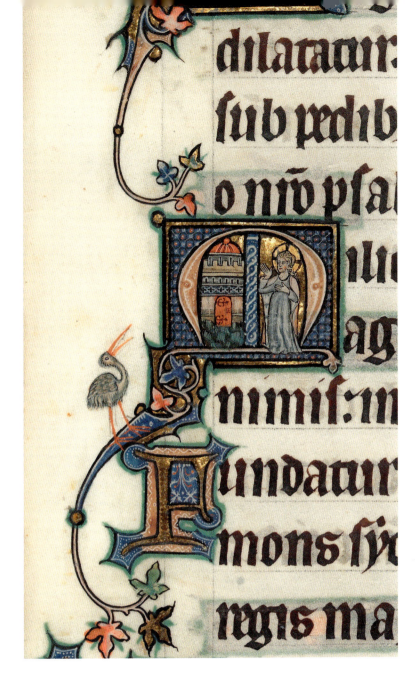

above the knight's sword (PLATE 9). He also left the spaces at the ends of the lines blank, to be completed by those artists to whom he distributed the quires, or as part of a later campaign.

Once he had finished illuminating the major pages, the Ormesby Master passed on various quires to other artists. The decoration in Section 5 (fols 58r–69v) was executed by an illuminator working in a decidedly Continental manner strongly reminiscent of that of another of the artists who worked on the de Bar manuscripts (FIGURE 42). In this section, as in Renaud's Breviary, now split between London and Verdun, psalm, collect and verse initials are set against deeply cusped

43 (*opposite*) Breviary of Renaud de Bar, Verdun, Bibliothèque municipale MS. 107, fol. 285v, before 1316.

44 M initial with Christ and the Heavenly Jerusalem. Psalm 47, Ormesby Psalter, 1310s campaign. Oxford, Bodleian Library MS. Douce 366, fol. 66r.

INTRODUCTION 59

...antur in velum 7 reueriantur:co
gitantes michi mala.

ferant confestim confusionem suam:
qui dicunt michi euge euge.

xultent 7 letentur super te omnes que
rentes te: 7 dicant semper magnificet
dominus qui diligunt salutare tuum.

go autem mendicus sum 7 pauper: do
minus sollicitus est mei.

diutor meus 7 protector meus tu es:
deus meus ne tardaueris.

xpectatio tuorum unica famu
lorum deus qui uenturum mun
do caput libri principalis edocuit: in
sere precamur legem in cordibz nris.
ut tuas iusticias nunciantes. abimi

panels, and small hooded bipeds, birds, fish and animals perch on elegant swinging tendrils in the margins (FIGURE 43). This artist adhered to the original decorative scheme of alternating historiated and decorated initials for psalms and collects. The psalm initials follow the French system and show King David acting out the opening words of the psalm, with the exception of Psalm 47 where David is replaced with Christ (FIGURE 44). Line fillers contain animals and zoomorphs, fish, foliage, and a wide variety of coats of arms, some Continental. Those of Warenne, Newmarch, Fitzalan and Clare are again prominent, while the royal arms of France (*azure* semé of fleur-de-lys *or*) appears on fol. 58r (FIGURE 45). Other coats previously thought to be purely decorative can be identified as those of the great *paraiges* of Metz, including Porte-Moselle (barry *or* and *azure),* Outre-Seille (chevronny of 8, *or* and *azure)* and Jurue (*d'or* aigle *sable*) (FIGURE 42).

The artist of Section 6 (fols 70r–81v) abandoned any attempt at figural imagery and confined himself to foliage decoration in the initials, with occasional grotesques and the arms of Clare in the line fillers (FIGURE 46). This decorator, whose style sits squarely in the mainstream of the Gorleston Psalter tradition, also contributed to the Stowe Breviary, made for use in the Diocese of Norwich and datable to between 1322 and 1325 (FIGURE 47). Later in his career he executed the minor decoration of the St Omer Psalter of *c*. 1330–40 (FIGURE 48).

Sections 7 to 13 were left blank during this campaign and hastily filled in later in the fourteenth century. The illuminator of Sections 14 and 17 (fols 154r–165v and fols 190r–201v) completed only a single page (FIGURE 17), and left delicate designs for slender borders and line fillers with the arms of the Bardolf and Foliot families on others (FIGURE 49). The decoration of these sections was a collaborative effort, with the master sketching in the outlines but leaving the simpler and more repetitive parts of the decoration to an assistant. It must have been abandoned suddenly: the distinctive orange and white vertical bar which runs behind the initials on fol. 154r has been only partially completed on some folios. Elsewhere gesso has been laid for gilding and parts of foliage painted (FIGURE 50). Similar bar borders with grotesques growing from the top are found

45 E initial with hare and magpie in border, collect to Psalm 39, Ormesby Psalter, 1310s campaign. Oxford, Bodleian Library MS. Douce 366, fol. 58r.

46 (*overleaf*) Ormesby Psalter, 1310s campaign. Oxford, Bodleian Library MS. Douce 366, fols 80v and 81r.

INTRODUCTION 61

Deduxisti me quia factus es spes mea: turris fortitudinis a facie inimici.
Inhabitabo in tabernaculo in secula: protegar in uelamento alarum tuarum.
Quoniam tu deus meus exaudisti orationem meam: dedisti hereditatem timentibus nomen tuum.
Dies super dies regis adicies: annos eius usque in diem generationis et generationis.
Permanet in eternum in conspectu dei mi sericordiam et ueritatem eius quis requiret.
Sic psalmum dicam nomini tuo in seculum seculi: ut reddam uota mea de die in diem.
Iniquitatum nostrarum miserisse consolator deus protege familiam tuam a facie inimici: ut arce turre fortitudinis premunita inhabitare tabernacula me

ratur eterna · per ·

onne deo subiecta erit anima me
a: ab ipo enim salutare meum·
am et ipe deus meus et salutaris meus:
susceptor meus non mouebor amplius·
uousq; irruitis in hominem interficit
uniuersi uos: tamquam parieti incli
nato et macerie depulse·

erumptamen precium meum cogita
uerunt repellere cucurri in siti: ore suo
benedicebant et corde suo maledicebant·

erumptamen deo subiecti esto anima
mea: qm ab ipo pacientia mea·

uia ipe deus meus et saluator meus: ad
iutor meus non emigrabo·

n deo salutare meum et gloria mea: de
us auxilii mei et spes mea in deo est·

perate in deo omnis egregatio populi

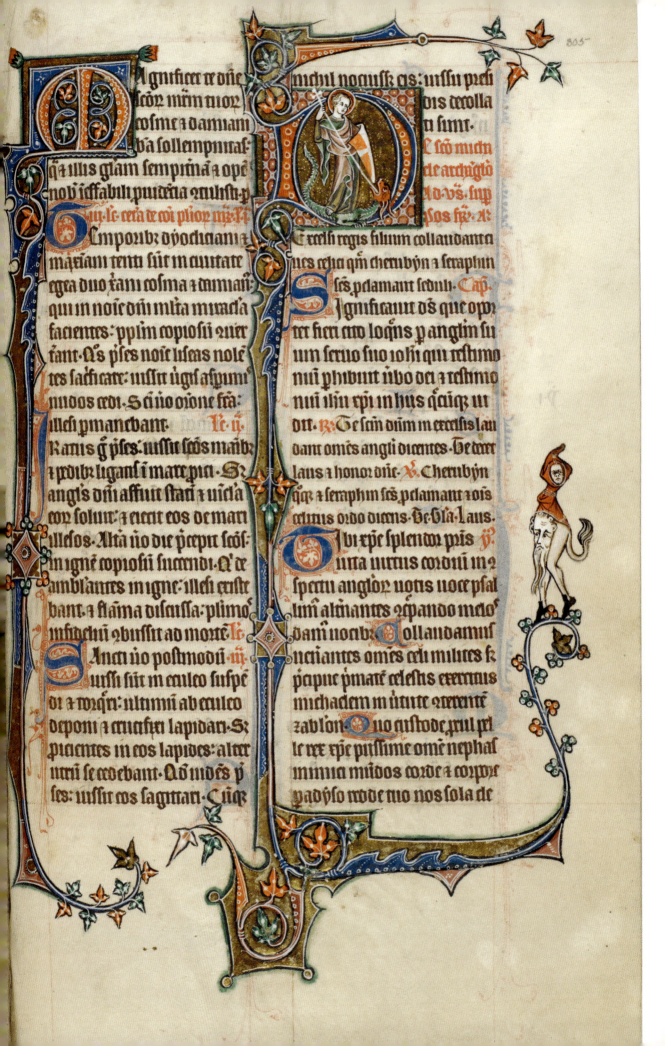

in the Vaux-Bardolf Psalter of *c.* 1300–1310 (FIGURE 51).[43] It has plausibly been suggested that these sections are the work of a member of an atelier who had been working for the Bardolfs elsewhere, and who was imported to speed up this campaign.[44]

In Section 17 gesticulating or grimacing figures growing from the tops of the bar borders are arranged in comic confrontations across many of the openings (FIGURE 52). Tendrils of flowering peas and pods, oak leaves and acorns swing across the lower margins of his pages. Sadly, all his drawings for psalm and collect initials have disappeared beneath subsequent overpainting, although his sketches for Bardolf, Foliot and Clare arms in the line fillers were followed by a later decorator, albeit roughly and in inappropriate colours. Aspects of this artist's style and *mise en page* link him with the workshop which produced the Howard Psalter and other manuscripts in the 1310s and 20s.[45]

The efficient division of labour practised in this campaign, with the decoration divided both hierarchically and physically among so many artists, suggests a desire for a glamorous

47 (*opposite*) Stowe Breviary, D initial, St Michael and the dragon. London, British Library Stowe MS. 12, fol. 305r, after 1322.

48 D initial with decorative border from the St Omer Psalter, *c.* 1330–40. London, British Library Yates Thompson MS. 14, fol. 8r.

INTRODUCTION 65

object produced at high speed. But why was it abandoned so abruptly, with the decoration only partially complete? The heraldic decoration offers clues as to the identity of its patrons, and it is their story which accounts for the incomplete state in which the manuscript was once more left. The evidence of the heraldry is not straightforward, however. Some of the shields refer to families who have no very evident connection with the Bardolfs and Foliots, while others seem to have had their tinctures altered for decorative effect. Moreover the range of heraldry in the line fillers varies from one section to another, suggesting a degree of independence on the part of the individual artists rather than a coherent programme. Such caveats aside, the most numerous shields reflect a web of personal and family allegiances between the Bardolfs, the Foliots and their immediate Norfolk circle, in particular their close connections with the Earls of Warenne.

Who were these families whose association with the Ormesby Psalter is repeatedly asserted through figural imagery and coats of arms? Why did they take up a partially illuminated manuscript, commission some of the most important and innovative artists of the age to complete it, then abandon the project unfinished? Large luxury psalters like the Ormesby Psalter were sometimes made to mark marriages or betrothals between aristocratic families, and double portraits of a man and a woman are generally understood as representing married couples. There is no record of a Foliot–Bardolf wedding in the early fourteenth century, but this does not mean that one never took place, or was at least planned. Medieval marriage was more a matter of family alliances than affection, and children could be betrothed to each other at a very early age. Such betrothals rarely appear in surviving records, especially if for some reason the proposed marriage failed to materialize. The Foliot man on the frontispiece is shown dressed not as a knight but in civilian clothes, perhaps indicating his status as a minor. Could the Ormesby Psalter have been intended to commemorate an early engagement and abandoned when it came to nothing? A closer look at the history of both families allows us a remarkable insight into the events and motivations surrounding the commissioning and sudden abandonment of work on this campaign.

49 Canticle of Isaiah, underdrawings from the 1310s campaign overpainted by Cheap Finisher. Oxford, Bodleian Library MS. Douce 366, fol. 190r.

66 THE ORMESBY PSALTER

temporalia relinquere. atqz ad eterna fe
stinare: da famulis tuis ut que a te iuf
sa cognouimus. implere celesti inspira
tione ualeamus. per.

Ego dixi in dimidio dierum meo
rum: uadam ad portas inferi.

Quesiui residuum annox tuox: dixi non
uidebo dnm deum in terra uiuentium.

Non aspiciam hominem ultra: 7 habitato
rem quietis.

Generatio mea ablata est 7 conuoluta e a me:
quasi tabernaculum pastorum.

Precisa est uelut a texente uita mea dum
adhuc ordirer succidit me: de mane usqz
ad uesperam finies me.

Sperabam usqz ad mane: quasi leo sic co
triuit omnia ossa mea.

De mane ad uesperam finies me: sicut

bulant in lege domini.

Beati qui scrutantur testimonia eius: in toto corde exquirunt eum.

Non enim qui operantur iniquitatem: in uiis eius ambulauerunt.

Tu mandasti: mandata tua custodiri nimis.

Utinam dirigantur uie mee: ad custodiendas iustificationes tuas.

Tunc non confundar: cum perspexero in omnibus mandatis tuis.

Confitebor tibi in directione cordis: in eo quod didici iudicia iustitie tue.

Iustificationes tuas custodiam: non me derelinquas usquequaque.

Deus qui custodis uitam adolescentium. uias corrigis. iusticiam doces. reuocas a peccatis. fac nos in testimon

iustus sicut in omnibus diuiciis delectan. p.

In quo corrigit adolescentior uiam suã:
in custodiendo sermones tuos.

In toto corde meo exquisiui te: ne repel
las me a mandatis tuis.

In corde meo abscondi eloquia tua: ut
non peccem tibi.

Benedictus es domine: doce me iustifica
tiones tuas.

In labiis meis: pronunciaui omnia iu
dicia oris mei.

In uia testimonior tuorum delectatus
sum: sicut in omnibus diuiciis.

In mandatis tuis exercebor: 7 considera
bo uias tuas.

In iustificationibus tuis meditabor: non
obliuiscar sermones tuos.

Retribue seruo tuo: uiuifica me 7

The Bardolf and Foliot family stories are intriguingly entwined, both with each other and with those great East Anglian magnates, the Earls of Warenne. Like the Warennes, the Bardolfs and the Foliots had origins in Normandy, and had arrived in England in the years immediately after the Norman Conquest. Both, moreover, moved in the same social circles. Not from the first rank of the aristocracy, they were nevertheless substantial landowners, with a history of bettering themselves through dedicated service to the Crown or the Church and through shrewd marriage.

The first recorded member of the Norfolk branch, the Barons Bardolf of Wormegay, was William Bardolf, sheriff of Norfolk and Suffolk from 1170 to 1175. By the late thirteenth century the family were well established on an upwardly mobile social path, having married a series of heiresses. They acquired the Honour of Wormegay, their main seat, via a Warenne bride in the early thirteenth century (see FAMILY TREE). They continued to hold large tracts of land in Norfolk from the Earls of Warenne and the Bishop of Norfolk as well as lands in Suffolk, Buckinghamshire, Derbyshire, Hertfordshire, Lincolnshire, Nottinghamshire, Suffolk and Yorkshire. The towns of Stow Bardolph in Norfolk and Stoke Bardolph in Nottinghamshire recall their widespread holdings in those counties.

The family's efforts at social elevation came to fruition in Hugh, the first Lord Bardolf (1259–1303/4), who was summoned to Parliament six times by the title 'Lord of Wirmegeye'. Hugh had served Edward I in Gascony and in his wars in Scotland in the 1300s. In 1300 he was part of a cavalry force whose visual effect was vividly described in the poem the 'Song of Caerlaverock', where Hugh himself was mentioned as 'a man of great appearance, rich, valiant and courteous'.[46] In his early twenties Hugh married an heiress, Isabella, sole daughter and heir of Sir Robert Aguillon of Addington, Surrey (now just outside Croydon) and Watton-at-Stone, Hertfordshire, and granddaughter of William de Ferrers, Earl of Derby. Hugh and Isabella had two sons, the elder Thomas, born in 1282, and the younger William, whose date of birth is unknown. A small insight into both the pleasures and the trials of the family's lifestyle is offered by the numerous complaints Hugh brought of poaching on his

50 (*previous spread*) Psalm 118, underdrawing and partial illumination from the Ormesby Psalter, 1310s campaign, overpainted by Cheap Finisher. Oxford, Bodleian Library Douce MS. Douce 366, fols 155v and 156r.

51 Vaux-Bardolf Psalter with bar border and grotesque terminal, *c.* 1310–20. London, Lambeth Palace Library MS. 233, fol. 23v.

Vt quid domine recessisti longe: despicis
in opportunitatibus in tribulatione.
Dum superbit impius incenditur pauper:
comprehenduntur in consiliis qui-
bus cogitant.
Quoniam lau- datur peccator in desi-
deriis anime sue: 7 iniquus benedi-
citur. Exacerbauit dominum peccator: secundum multitudinem ire
sue non queret.
Non est deus in conspectu eius: in qui-
nate sunt uie illius in omni tempore.
Auferuntur iudicia tua a facie eius: 7
omnium inimicorum suorum dominabit.
Dixit enim in corde suo: non mouebor
a generatione in generationem sine
malo.

rcus fortiü supauis ē·7 infirmi accincti
sunt roboze· ·

Repleti pprius p panibz se locauerunt·7 fa
melica saturati sunt·

Donec sterilis pepent plurimos·7 que mt
tos habebat filios infirmata est·

Dominus mortificat 7 uiuificat·7 deducit
ad inferos 7 reducit·

Dñs pauperē facit 7 ditat· humiliat 7 subliat·

Suscitans de puluere egenum·7 de stercore
erigens pauperem·

Et sedeat cum principibz·7 solium glorie
teneat·

Domini enim sunt cardines terre·7 posu
it super eos orbem·

Pedes sctorum suorum seruabit 7 impii i
tenebris conticescent·quia non in fortitu
dine sua roborabitur uir·

nim formidabunt aduersarii eius:7 super
ipos in celis tonabit.

nis iudicabit fines terre 7 dabit impiu regi
suo:7 sullimabit cornu xpi sui.

mips sempiterne ds spes unica mu
di. qui apphetay ora precomo pre
sentium tempoy declarasti miseriam:
auge populi tui uota placatus.quia i
nullo fidelium nisi ex tua inspiratoe
quaxlibet incresinta uirtutu puemut.p.

antemus dno glose enim honori
ficatus est:equum 7 ascensorem
deiecit in mare.

ortitudo mea 7 laus mea dominus:7 fac
tus e michi in salutem.

ste deus meus 7 honorificabo eum: deus
patris mei 7 exaltabo.

nis quasi uir pugnator omps nomen e.

Norfolk estates during his frequent absences. These included incidents of breaking and entering at Stow Bardolph, and the theft of sparrowhawks, herons, spoonbills and bitterns (all birds raised for hawking and for the table, much as pheasants are today raised for shooting) in woods at Whinburgh and elsewhere, and swans at Wormegay. These accusations were heard by William de Ormesby, local justice and father of Robert, the monk who gave his name to the Ormesby Psalter. The Aguillons also had land interests in Scratby, next to Ormesby on the Norfolk coast, where they owned Aguillons Hall and a manor known as Scratby Bardolphs, while 3 miles inland from Ormesby the Vaux family held a manor at Fleggburgh. The manors are so closely associated that rentals and court records for Ormesby, Scratby Bardolphs and Burgh Vaux are listed together in post-medieval records. The interconnections between these bibliophile Norwich gentry are fascinating.

Hugh was dead by August 1304, too early to have played a direct role in the commissioning of the Ormesby Psalter. Isabella survived her husband by almost twenty years, and even through the dark glass of medieval records gives the impression of a redoubtable character. Well provided for by her family, with a considerable annual income from rents and the advowsons on several churches, she lived until 1323, appointing clerks to represent her in chancery, lending money and vigorously pursuing several lawsuits throughout the 1310s. If not directly concerned herself in the commissioning of the Ormesby Psalter, she at least was a powerful presence in the lives of those who were: her son Thomas, his wife and their children. She certainly knew and had dealings with the Foliot family. Richard Foliot held a knight's fee at Mendham in Suffolk from her, and a land assessment of 1316 lists among her tenants one Margaret (an alternative spelling of the name Margery) Folyot, another long-lived widow, *que fuit uxor Jordani Folyot* (who was the wife of Jordan Foliot).

The two families' connections went back much further than this, however. The fortunes of the Norfolk branch of the Foliot family were founded in the early thirteenth century when one Richard Foliot married one of the five sisters of Robert Bardolf (d. 1225) (see FAMILY TREE). This Robert was the brother and

52 (*previous spread*) Canticle of Habbakuk, Ormesby Psalter, 1310s campaign. Oxford, Bodleian Library MS. Douce 366, fols 194v and 195r.

74 THE ORMESBY PSALTER

heir of Hugh Bardolf, the justice of Richard I. When both Hugh and Robert died childless, Hugh's great estates were split between the sisters, the Foliot family acquiring the manor of Hoo in Kent. Jordan, the first Lord Foliot, was well acquainted with his Bardolf neighbours: an undated document from the reign of Henry III (1216–72) transferring land from Jordan to his brother William was witnessed first by William Bardolf and secondly by Roger de Vaux, a representative of another family known for its manuscript patronage.

The Foliot family reached their apogee in the late thirteenth and early fourteenth centuries. Richard Foliot (d. March 1299) married Margery d'Estuteville, by whom he had two sons, Jordan and William. The elder became the first Lord Foliot when called to Parliament in 1295. Like his contemporary Hugh Bardolf, Jordan played a minor but active part in both war and politics, participating in Edward I's military campaigns in Wales and in Scotland in the 1290s under his feudal overlord, the Earl of Warenne. He married a Yorkshire heiress, Margery de Newmarch, by whom he had at least two children, a son Richard and a daughter Beatrice. Jordan held lands in Derby-shire, Nottinghamshire and Yorkshire, but his main estate was the great manor of Gressenhall in Norfolk, held of the Earl of Warenne. Other lands in Norfolk, including Elsing, Guist and Twyford, were held of the Earls of Gloucester. Jordan died before 2 May 1299, less than five weeks after his father Richard, but Margery lived on into the 1330s and was buried before the high altar at Wendling Abbey, less than 3 miles from Gressen-hall. Another strong-minded widow, she hung on to a good portion of her son's inheritance, retaining six of the ten manors of his inheritance in jointure and dower until her death.

By the beginning of the fourteenth century, then, both families might well have been feeling a certain degree of satisfaction, if not complacency, with their respective positions and prospects. Both had recently achieved a major elevation in social status, the Foliot barony having been written in 1295 by Sir Jordan Foliot, while Hugh Bardolf had become the first Lord Bardolf in 1299. By this step both families had gone from being members of the gentry (knights and esquires with incomes of up to £200 per annum who could be elected to Parliament as

INTRODUCTION   75

53 The remains of Castle Acre, Norfolk, seat of the Warennes.

knights of the shires) to being part of the parliamentary peerage (the seventy or so families with hereditary rights to be called to Parliament). Both had considerable estates across central and eastern England, were important members of the Norfolk elite and held neighbouring land around Dereham. More importantly for our understanding of the Ormesby Psalter, both were closely connected with one of the most powerful men in the kingdom, John de Warenne, the last Earl of Surrey and Suffolk.

The main seats of the Bardolfs at Wormegay and the Foliots at Gressenhall both lie within 5 miles of the Warennes' great castle at Castle Acre (FIGURE 53 and MAP), and both held their land in tenure from the earls. The Warennes would have been important figures in the lives of the Foliots in particular. Richard Foliot, son of Sir Jordan, was born before 25 December 1283 and so was still a minor at his father's death in 1299. According to the complex laws of child custody and medieval inheritance, if a child inherited property while under the age

76 THE ORMESBY PSALTER

of majority and if that land was held in military tenure, the wardship belonged to the lord from whom the land was held. Richard, therefore, was placed in the custody of the Earls of Clare and Warenne, but seems to have lived with John, 6th Earl of Warenne, as his mother was trying unsuccessfully to get him back from the earl in the year after his father's death. He doubtless spent the next few years either at the earl's court at Castle Acre, or travelling with him.

Also with the earl was his grandson, another John, who had been born in June 1286. Young John's father, William, had been accidentally killed in a tournament at Croydon six months before his son's birth and his mother died when he was 7. The orphan heir was only three years younger than Richard, and the two must have been companions. Growing up in the sophisticated environment of the old earl's household would have been an educative experience for both boys. The family had a house in London at the south end of London Bridge as well as various country properties, and the earl had his own organist.

After the death of his grandfather in 1304, the young John became a royal ward. Orphan heirs in the king's wardship were generally brought up at court, along with the royal children and others sent there for that purpose, and from this point John presumably resided at least in part at the royal court. In the fifteenth century the court was described as 'the chief academy for the nobility of England, and a school for athletics, morals and manners', but the words could equally well have been written a hundred years earlier. It is conceivable that Richard Foliot was also at court by this time. The king had claimed the wardship for himself in 1301, though this was contested by tenants from across the Foliot estates in Norfolk, Suffolk, Cambridgeshire and Kent, as well as those from Nottinghamshire and Yorkshire, and Warenne succeeded in retaining it, at least for the present.

Certainly both were at Westminster in May 1306 for the knighting of Prince Edward, later Edward II. To celebrate this event, 267 men were knighted in Westminster Abbey, among them the 23-year-old Richard Foliot and the 20-year-old John de Warenne. Along with them was a third, 24-year old Thomas, the second Lord Bardolf. Given the large numbers of men at the Whitsuntide dubbing, we should perhaps not read too much into the presence of representatives of the two families involved in the Ormesby Psalter. Intriguingly, however, Thomas Bardolf had also been a ward at the royal court at the same time as John de Warenne. Thomas was born on St Francis Day (4 October) 1282, at his maternal grandfather's estates at Watton-at-Stone. After his father's death in 1304, the rights to arrange his marriage and the profit from his lands were granted to Margaret, Queen of England. This was an odd arrangement given Thomas's age, and apparently little to Thomas's liking. In November 1304 the Calendar of Chancery Warrants recorded

> Mandate, as the king has offered to Thomas, son and heir of Sir Hugh Bardolf, a suitable marriage, and he has refused the king's offer and answered that he does not wish to be married, and it seems to the king that this answer is insufficient and it may be a bad example for the king and his heirs and all to whom he wishes to do well, if heirs in the king's marriage are suffered to excuse themselves and refuse the marriages offered by the king, to be as stiff and hard towards Thomas in this business as can be without offending the law.

The canny old Edward I had perhaps seized the opportunity to get his hands on a profitable estate and arrange a marriage to suit him before the heir, although of age, had a chance to do homage. By December Thomas had come into his inheritance.

John de Warenne and Thomas certainly knew each other well, as Thomas held a considerable part of his lands in feudal tenure from the earl. Bardolf's arms are included in the Gorleston Psalter, made for Warenne in the 1310s or 1320s, and gold Bardolf cinquefoils also appear on the Thornham Parva Retable. John de Warenne probably acted as godfather to Thomas's son, who was named John and who became Warenne's ward on Thomas's death in 1328.

At the very least, then, in Thomas Bardolf, Richard Foliot and John de Warenne we have a triumvirate of three young men, all from within a 10-mile radius of each other in Norfolk, all at court in their early twenties, with long-standing family connections, and linked through the ties of feudal tenure and friendship. Even on its own this is a fascinating grouping, but it is possible to speculate further. Warenne was part of a group of educated, intelligent and literate young men at court, a group which gathered around the then Prince Edward. Were Thomas and Richard also part of this group, or at least on its fringes?

Certainly both Thomas and Richard maintained an almost unbroken record of loyalty to Edward II throughout the turbulent rule of that troubled and troublesome king, as did John de Warenne himself. After the death of Edward I in 1307, Richard Foliot flourished as a trusted and valued servant of the new regime. He was sent abroad on the king's service in January 1308 and on 6 September 1310 was granted the marriage of Joan, widow of James de Bohun. Joan was the younger daughter and co-heir of William de Brewes, Lord of Bamber and Gower, one of the Marcher Lords and the last of a great family. In spite of the political upheavals and natural disasters through which they lived – famine and pestilence followed a ruined harvest in 1315, with the consequent inflation in prices of basic foods increasing the hardship, and leading one chronicler to speak of misery 'such as our age has never seen' – Richard and Joan succeeded in raising a promising family. Three children are recorded: a son and heir, also Richard, presumably born in 1311 or 1312, and two daughters, the elder, Margery, born in 1313 and the younger, Margaret, born in 1314. The fortunes of the family were flourishing, and the death of the father on the king's service in Scotland, possibly at Bannockburn in June 1314, must have been a great blow. What happened to his young family at this point is vital to our understanding of the Ormesby Psalter. Although their mother, Joan, lived on until 1324, according to the laws of feudal tenure her three children became the wards of their father's feudal overlord, the selfsame John de Warenne with whom Richard had grown up.

Thomas Bardolf's personal life seems to have been equally satisfactory, although relatively short: he died in 1328 aged 46. His wife Agnes, who lived until 1357, was described as born 'in parts of Almain' and was perhaps the daughter of William de Grandson, Seigneur of Grandson on Lake Neuchâtel, now in Switzerland. Their eldest son, John, was born in January 1311 and married Elizabeth d'Amory, granddaughter of Gilbert de

INTRODUCTION   79

Clare, who brought with her the bulk of the Honor of Clare in East Anglia, as well as vast estates in Dorset. The names are known of two other sons, Edmund and Thomas, and one daughter, Cecily, who married William Lord Morley. As with the Foliots, the wardship of Thomas's children on his death passed in part to John de Warenne as his feudal overlord. Was Warenne responsible for arranging the series of betrothals of Bardolf children seemingly celebrated in surviving psalters? In addition to the Vaux–Bardolf Psalter in Lambeth, a Psalter in the Escorial contains the Bardolf and Bussey arms, although no marriages between these families are recorded in the medieval documents.[47]

Thomas Bardolf's record of service to Edward II more than equalled that of Richard Foliot. Aside from one brief flirtation with Lancastrianism in the early 1320s, the most conspicuous feature of his public career is his loyalty to a difficult monarch in difficult times. In 1308 he attended Edward's coronation. He was summoned to Parliament almost thirty times from 26 August 1307 to 23 October 1330, and throughout the late 1310s and early 1320s he acted as a commissioner and keeper of the peace in Norfolk and Suffolk. He was charged with raising both cavalry and infantry forces for Edward II's campaigns in Scotland in 1317 and 1321, and fighting for the king against the rebels there in 1321.

He continued to stand by the king through the deepening crises of the 1320s. By 1325 Thomas was preparing to defend the seashores against the expected invasion of Edward's rebellious wife Queen Isabella and her lover Roger Mortimer, and in 1326 was appointed Chief Inspector of Array and Conservator of the Peace for Norfolk. The king spent Christmas 1326 at Bury St Edmunds, and went from there to Norwich. Thomas was perhaps among his retinue. After the deposition of Edward II in January 1327, nothing more is heard of Thomas until the *inquisitio post mortem* into his death before 15 December 1328. His lack of involvement with the new Mortimer government perhaps reflected his close association with the previous regime.

Such loyalty to the king could perhaps be explained in part by an intense if brief experience of court life, and of the young and sophisticated circle around the then Prince Edward.

Certainly the Bardolf family were intimately acquainted with courtly modes of patronage, which they aped by commissioning a group of luxury psalters of the kind that were customarily made to mark the marriages of royalty and the *haute aristocratie*.

The Bardolfs' patronage of deluxe psalters did more than imitate the customs of the aristocracy which they had so recently joined. It was perhaps most immediately inspired and even encouraged by their neighbour and feudal overlord John de Warenne, who is emerging as one of the most important English patrons of the first half of the fourteenth century. Patron of the Priories at Castle Acre and at Lewes, he has recently been identified as commissioner of both the Gorleston and Macclesfield Psalters, with which the Ormesby Psalter shares many features of style and iconography, and of the Thornham Parva Retable, whose style is a later version of that of the Ormesby Master. It was perhaps more than just a case of keeping up with the Warennes. On the death of Richard Foliot, John de Warenne had become guardian to his orphaned children. The first duty of a guardian was to arrange a suitable match for his ward. Can we speculate that John might have promoted a match between the young Lord Foliot, his ward and the son of a man with whom he had grown up, and the daughter of his feudal tenant and friend, Thomas Bardolf?

If this were the case, the reason why the Ormesby Psalter was so suddenly abandoned becomes clear. Despite his best efforts, Warenne's custody of the infant Richard Foliot did not last long. The wardship was one of great value (the estates at Gressenhall and Weasenham alone were respectively valued at £40 and £18 annually in 1325), and became the subject of a court case between John de Warenne and Thomas, Earl of Lancaster. Lancaster's feud with Warenne had escalated into war after Lancaster interfered in Warenne's attempts to obtain a divorce. In 1317 Lancaster's wife was either abducted by Warenne, or alternatively left her husband and sought asylum with Warenne, depending on which version of the story you prefer. Warenne came off worst in this conflict. From November 1318 to March 1319 he was coerced into a series of punishing settlements with Lancaster, by which he was forced to release his estates across Yorkshire, North Wales and Norfolk to the earl, along with the

INTRODUCTION 81

wardship of Richard Foliot. With his loss of the wardship, his plans for the young Richard's future marriage collapsed and with them the *raison d'être* for his involvement with the decoration of the Ormesby Psalter.

What of the children whose planned betrothal was so richly commemorated in the manuscript? The Bardolf family continued to prosper well into the next century, but the fortunes of the Foliots were now in decline. Richard Foliot was a childless minor when he died on 29 May 1325, by which time he was married to Elizabeth Segrave (d. 1338), daughter of John, Lord Segrave. The Segrave family were close associates of Thomas of Lancaster. Steven Segrave was one of the twelve of Lancaster's retainers who witnessed the 1318 charter by which Warenne was forced to hand over his inheritance to Lancaster, and Nicholas Segrave was described by Lancaster in a document of 1318 as 'his well-loved companion'.[48] With Richard's death the barony died out, and his lands then passed to his two sisters, Margery, aged 12, and Margaret, aged 13. The wardship of these two young heiresses was essentially sold by the king to Isabel de Hastings and John de Camoys respectively, who promptly married them off to their own children. The Foliot estates were divided between the two sisters, but eventually reverted to the children of Margery and Sir Hugh de Hastings after Margaret died without issue. Margery at least continued the tradition of artistic patronage which was such a feature of the Warenne court where she had in part grown up. With her husband, Sir Hugh de Hastings (d. 1347/8), she rebuilt the church at Elsing, and was depicted with him in the stained glass there.[49] She also perhaps commissioned his tomb, the grand brass of which survives in the church.[50]

But the dynastic security and prosperity which the Foliots had spent generations building had evaporated, and in their case the words of Psalm 1, which originally ran across the Jesse frontispiece, now seem sadly misplaced:

> And he shall be like a tree which is planted near running waters,
>   which shall bring forth its fruit in due season.
> And his leaf shall not fall off, and all whatsoever he shall do
>   shall prosper.

The Foliots had become instead, in the words of that psalm, 'like the dust, which the wind driveth from the face of the earth'.

The 1330s campaign: Robert of Ormesby and Norwich Cathedral Priory

Once more abandoned unfinished, the unbound quires of the manuscript perhaps lay on the shelf of a stationer's or illuminator's workshop for as much as two decades before being picked up by its next patron, Robert of Ormesby, monk of Norwich. He set in motion a series of adaptations to render the book suitable for use at his home institution.

Removing the original Calendar, he had it replaced with one reflecting the liturgical practices of Norwich Cathedral (FIGURE 54). The new Calendar includes the feast of the Dedication of the Cathedral in gold (24 September) along with its Octave (1 October) and the Translation of the Norwich Relics (16 September). There are also various Norwich saints, among them Bonitus (15 January); Felix of Dunwich, first bishop of East Anglia (8 March); William of Norwich, the boy-martyr whose body was buried in the Martyr's Chapel in the Cathedral (24 March); Ethelbert, an eighth-century king of the East Angles (20 May); Neot (31 July); Osyth, to whom a chapel in the Cathedral was dedicated (7 October); and the translation of Etheldreda (17 October).

The feasts are graded in importance by colour, with ordinary feasts in red and more important feasts in blue or gold. In general those feasts which according to the Norwich Customary[51] were celebrated *in capis* or *in albis* (i.e. those days when the community would appear at High Mass vested in copes or albs) appear in blue. Feasts in gold are those which were particularly liturgically elaborate, either the great feasts of the Christian Church such as Christmas and Epiphany, or the feasts of the Virgin. These were especially important at Norwich after the building of the Lady Chapel behind the High Altar in the middle of the thirteenth century. Feasts of saints with chapels in Norwich Cathedral are also singled out. The feasts of the Nativity of St John the Baptist and Saints Peter and Paul are in gold, while those of Saints Thomas of Canterbury, Catherine, Andrew, Edmund and Stephen are in blue, as is St Benedict (Norwich was a Benedictine institution).

On the back of the last leaf of the Calendar is an erased version of the dedication inscription (FIGURE 55). This second

INTRODUCTION   83

inscription contrasts strongly with the professional version at the beginning of the manuscript. As well as small differences in orthography, it is written in cursive, a less formal script, by an amateur scribe who used inconsistent letter forms and variable letter sizes. The mix of thirteenth- and fourteenth-century letterforms suggests someone who learned to write in the late thirteenth century, and continued to use some older forms in combination with new introductions. Could this inscription have been written in by Robert himself, who was born in the late thirteenth century and, as subprior, must have continued to have to write throughout his career?

The original Litany could not be removed as it was contiguous with the text of the Canticles on fol. 206v. Instead, the Norwich scribe simply began a new Litany after the end of the original Petitions on fol. 209r. In the second Litany, William of Norwich receives a capital letter and a double invocation (FIGURE 56). St Benedict also has a double invocation. The Litany is followed by a long list of petitions, including requests for blessings upon kings and princes, bishops and abbots and all their congregations, and upon 'this house and all its inhabitants'. Finally there are thirteen collects, very similar to those found after the added Norwich litany in the Gorleston Psalter.

Robert also commissioned important modifications to the decorative programme. Rather than discard folio 10 and replace it with the single leaf showing the Jesse Tree, Robert chose to adapt the frontispiece with the addition of the figures of the monk and the bishop over the lines of text. The same artist painted the large initial of David enthroned at the beginning of the first psalm (PLATE 2). This illuminator, known as the St Omer Master from his work in a psalter made for William de St Omer (d. 1347) of Mulbarton, Norfolk (FIGURE 57), also contributed to the Gorleston Psalter, decorating the reverse side of the Crucifixion added to that manuscript possibly after its arrival at Norwich. His style is representative of the Italianate phase of East Anglian illumination, when artists adopted painting techniques for the modelling of flesh and draperies derived from Sienese art.

Finally, in order to render the manuscript suitable for use in church, Robert had the book bound. The quires were sewn

54 September, with the feast of the Dedication of Norwich Cathedral in gold, Ormesby Psalter, 1330s campaign. Oxford, Bodleian Library MS. Douce 366, fol. 6r.

Tercia septembris z den fert mala membris.

xvi	f	KL	September. Sci egidij abb. s. prisci m̄.
v	g	iiij	
	a	iij	Ordinacio sci gregorij pape.
xiij	b	ij	
ij	c	Nonas	Finis caniculariū dier.
	d	viij	id
x	e	vij	id
	f	vi	id Nativitas scē marie virginis.
xviij	g	v	id Sci gorgonij m̄.
vij	a	iiij	id
	b	iij	id Scōr prothi z iacincti m̄.
xv	c	ij	id
iiij	d	Idus	
	e	xviij	kl Octobris. Exaltacio scē crucis. de ñb3 Sol
xij	f	xvij	kl Oct. scē marie. s. nichomedis m̄. in libra
j	g	xvi	kl Translo reliquiaȝ. s. eufemie virgis.
	a	xv	kl
ix	b	xiiij	kl
	c	xiij	kl
xvij	d	xij	kl Vigilia.
vi	e	xi	kl Sci mathei apli z euāgeliste.
	f	x	kl Sci mauricij socior qͥ eꝰ. m̄r.
xiiij	g	ix	kl
iij	a	viij	kl Dedicacio ecclie scē trinitatis Norwic.
	b	vij	kl
xi	c	vi	kl
xix	d	v	kl Scōr cosme z damiani m̄r.
	e	iiij	kl
viij	f	iij	kl Sci michaelis archangli.
	g	ij	kl Sci ieronimi presbit.

Ad iscundim cozam Saluoze quid ꝓ tempe
fuꝿt myesiam

to supports, and enclosed in wooden boards, which were then presumably covered with tawed skin – that is, skin which had been prepared by being immersed in a solution of alum. As noted above, the current binding, although medieval, is not the manuscript's first. A close examination of the inside back cover offers clues as to what the earlier binding looked like (FIGURE 58). Visible on the inside of the back cover are two holes for pins. These would have formed the connecting points for straps coming from the front cover of the book at a phase in the binding's history prior to the addition of the chemise. These pins, themselves no longer extant, pierced the outer folios of the final quire which form the flyleaf and paste-down. This quire contains the added Norwich Litany, associating this phase in the binding's history with Norwich Cathedral. Pins for straps like these were generally placed roughly symmetrically in the covers of bindings. The holes for straps in the Ormesby Psalter's back cover are considerably closer to the spine-edge than to the fore-edge, however, indicating that the boards themselves have been reused, and were cut down unevenly to fit their current position. When given to Norwich, the Psalter must have been somewhat larger than it is now, and bound with a binding closed by two straps.

Once bound, the book was presumably placed in the cathedral church at the place in the stalls reserved for the subprior, as laid down in the donation inscription. It was perhaps at this point that the earlier of the manuscript's two pressmarks was written on the first page of the Calendar. The Psalter has two Norwich pressmarks, A.1 enclosed in a box at the top centre of fol. 2r, and a second, partially erased mark [ ]xlij in the outer border (FIGURE 59). This can only be the result of two attempts at cataloguing, or at least making an inventory of the Norwich books for stocktaking purposes.

In the Norwich system of shelf marks, books from forty years or so after the 1272 fire bear a letter mark and inscription of ownership, identifying the donor. It has been argued that when this system was introduced older books which had survived the fire were given shelf mark A.[52] This cannot apply to the Ormesby Psalter, however, which was not given to the Cathedral until the 1330s. Surviving books containing the

55 The erased donation inscription on the Ormesby Psalter. Oxford, Bodleian Library MS. Douce 366, fol. 8v.

INTRODUCTION 87

'A' pressmark are either psalters or collections of sermons or homilies. 'A' seems to have been used to denote books kept in the church or in the refectory rather than in the book cupboards around the cloister, and thus includes some which escaped the 1272 destruction of the cloister books.[53] Although no fourteenth-century inventory of Norwich books now survives, the Precentor's roll refers to money spent in 1313–15 on producing a catalogue, and even books kept in the cathedral or elsewhere in the monastery must have been included for the purposes of stocktaking. The erasure of the old pressmark and the prominent insertion of 'A.1' indicate that when a new inventory was made the Ormesby Psalter was the first of the service books listed in the monastery's collection, or perhaps simply that it was regarded as Norwich's best manuscript.[54]

Who was the man who gave his name to one of the most splendid pieces of English medieval art? Robert of Ormesby is a surprisingly obscure figure, neither knight, nor courtier nor eminent ecclesiastic. He took no part in the turbulent politics of the day. He was never called upon to advise kings or princes. So far as we know he moved almost entirely within a small geographical range, rarely leaving East Anglia. The second son of a prosperous Norfolk family, he appears to have lived an entirely unremarkable life, pursuing a successful but uneventful career in provincial monastic administration. If it were not for the extraordinary manuscript which now bears his name, he would doubtless have sunk into total oblivion.

Like the Bardolfs and Foliots, the Ormesby family were landed gentry and professional administrators rather than aristocrats. As the name suggests, they had strong local connections. Ormesby is situated on the coast of Norfolk, about 5 miles north of Great Yarmouth (see MAP). Robert's father, Sir William de Ormesby, was an itinerant justice who played an important role in Edward I's Scottish policy. He was appointed a justice in the newly conquered Scotland in 1296 and gained a reputation for unflinching severity in exacting homage from the Scottish tenants-in-chief. He continued to function as a judge under Edward II and was a prominent local figure, acting as senior assize justice for Norfolk and Suffolk from 1308 to his death in 1317.

56 The second Litany, with double invocation of William of Norwich and St Benedict. Ormesby Psalter, 1330s campaign. Oxford, Bodleian Library MS. Douce 366, fol. 210r.

Sce corneli: or   Sce ambrosi: or
Sce cypriane: or   Sce augustine: or
Sce dyonisi cu soc or   Sce ieronime: or
Sce maurici c soc or   Sce basili: or
Sce eustachi c soc or   Sce gregori: or
Sce cyriace c soc or   Sce augustine c soc or
Sce sebastiane: or   Sce Nicholae: or
Sce xpofore: or   Sce audoene: or
Sce albane: or   Sce dunstane: or
Sce oswalde: or   Sce cuthberte: or
Sce edmunde: or   Sce felix: or
Sce elphege: or   Sce iuliane: or
Sce thoma: or   Sce bonite: or
Sce blasi: or   Sce edmunde: or
Sce wille ij. or   Sce benedicte ij. or
Oes sci mres or   Sce maure: or
Sce siluester: or   Sce leonarde: or
Sce marcialis: or   Sce paule: or
Sce taurine: or   Sce antoni: or
Sce hylari: or   Sce egidi: or
Sce martine: or   Sce nicote: or

Robert was probably the second of three sons born to William and his first wife, a local heiress named Agnes. The eldest, John, was married by 1294 and attended Parliament as MP for Norfolk between 1325 and 1334. He briefly held the post of sheriff of Norfolk and Suffolk in 1338, but his career was otherwise unremarkable. In the tradition of the landed gentry until relatively recently, both the younger boys went into the Church. William became rector of Witton in 1321 and of Holveston in 1356, both in Norfolk. Robert's career seems to have been more successful. Very little is known of his childhood, although what evidence there is suggests a close and stable family background. He was born before 1294, when his father settled land on all three of his sons, perhaps to mark the eldest's marriage. Sir William seems to have been an affectionate father. In addition to taking steps to provide for his children financially, he took John and Robert with him to Scotland in 1296, so Robert was presumably no longer an infant by this time. This was perhaps a more exciting introduction to the political problems of the day than they bargained for. In May 1297 the Scots rose against the occupying English, and William Wallace led an attack against Sir William while he was holding a session at Scone. Sir William lost all his personal possessions in the attack and was lucky to escape with his life. He fled back to England, presumably taking his sons with him.

On their return from Scotland, Robert was sent to the abbey of St Benet's, of which his father was a benefactor. Monastic institutions often acted as schools for local children, especially those planning to take monastic vows, and in 1299 the abbey presented Robert to the rectory of North Walsham as a chaplain. Although the position implied some religious duties, chaplains were not necessarily adults. Indeed benefices could be bestowed on clerics as early as their seventh year. Again, the family seems to have valued proximity. Both St Benet's and North Walsham lie within a few miles of the village of Ormesby. From there Robert went on to university to read theology or canon law, presumably at Gloucester College,

57 (*opposite*) Initial D with David enthroned debating with a fool, from the St Omer Psalter, Psalm 52, *c.* 1330–40. London, British Library Yates Thompson MS. 14, fol. 57v. (*above*) Initial B, Ormesby Psalter. Oxford, Bodleian Library MS. Douce 366, fol. 10r.

Oxford, a foundation with which Norwich was closely associated. From the late thirteenth century the great Benedictine houses were actively promoting university education for their young recruits and a relatively high proportion of Norwich monks were university educated.[55] There is no record of his graduating, but he must have done so, as he is referred to as 'Magister' in July 1323 when he, his brother and other Norwich clerks were involved in a fracas at Cambridge with the Bishop of Ely's men.[56]

After university, Robert returned to his home county of Norfolk, to the Cathedral Priory at Norwich. The next we hear of him is in 1334, by which time he was prior of Hoxne, near Diss in Suffolk. Hoxne was a small religious house comprising a prior and seven or eight monks, who ran a school for children of the parish. It was a cell of Norwich Cathedral and the prior was appointed by the prior of Norwich, so Robert must have become a monk at Norwich by this time. There was a long-standing connection between the Cathedral Priory and the Ormesby family. Not only did the Priory hold land at Ormesby, but Robert's father had acted as the prior's legal adviser in the 1280s, and the family made donations to the Priory in the 1290s and 1300s. Norwich must have seemed the obvious place for Robert after he had completed his education. By the time he became prior of Hoxne he had almost certainly also become a priest, as most monks who entered Norwich Cathedral Priory progressed through minor orders and were ordained once they reached the age of 25.

Robert's role as prior of Hoxne was something of a cross between headmaster and bursar (the monks ran a small school and the priors were bound to make annual returns to Norwich of their accounts), experience which would have stood him in good stead for his next position. In 1336/7 his name appears in Communar and Pittancer rolls of the Priory, as being given 66s 8d by the communar *ad opus elect* – for the election of Thomas of Hemenhale to the bishopric. Together with the reference to the subprior in the inscription in the front of the Ormesby Psalter, this strongly suggests that he had by this time risen to become subprior of the Cathedral Priory, a very senior position within the cathedral administration.

58 Ormesby Psalter, inside of back cover. Oxford, Bodleian Library MS. Douce 366.

92 THE ORMESBY PSALTER

ma dies mensis z septima truncatur ensis

		KL	Januarius. Circumcisio dni .j.
iii	a		
	b	iiii	Octaue sancti stephi prothomris.
ix	c	iii	Octaue sancti Iohis apli z ell ing
	d	ij	Octaue sanctor Innocencium. aix.
xix	e	Nonas	oct. Vigilia.
viii	f	viii	Epiphania domini. prm. f.
	g	vii	Claues. lxx.
xvi	a	vi	
v	b	v	
	c	iiii	
xiii	d	iij	
ij	e	ij	
	f	idus	Octaue epiphie. Sci hillarij. qf.
x	g	xix	februarij Sca felicis epi. Solin anno.
	a	xviii	Sca mauri epi. z sci mauri abbis.
xviii	b	xvii	Sca marcelli
vii	c	xvi	
	d	xv	Sca prisce uirginis.
xv	e	xiiii	
iiii	f	xiii	Sci seduastiani. aix. z sca fabiani. aix.
	g	xij	Sca Agnetis uirginis z aix.
xij	a	xi	Sca uincenci. aix.
j	b	x	
	c	ix	
ix	d	viii	Conuersio sci pauli...

The Holy Trinity at Norwich was a cathedral monastery; that is, a Benedictine monastery whose inmates performed the offices in the cathedral church, and where the role of abbot was fulfilled by the bishop. In practice, the political and administrative demands upon medieval bishops were such that the administration of cathedral monasteries almost always devolved upon the second in command. John Salmon, Bishop of Norwich 1299–1325, was also chancellor from 1310. Indeed, at Norwich, the prior had been in complete day-to-day control since the late twelfth century, presiding at chapter meetings and keeping a grip on the monastery's finances. The subprior was third in this chain of command, and was appointed by the bishop on the advice of the prior.

Unlike the obedientiaries (other monastic officials such as the librarian and cellarer), the subprior had no special function within the community, but the post was one of considerable responsibility, requiring both diplomacy and education. In the absence of the prior all his duties devolved upon the subprior. He was often in charge of disciplinary and financial matters, collecting and distributing certain funds and acting as a channel for transactions between the prior and the other obedientiaries (hence his collection of money for the election of a new bishop).

The Holy Trinity at Norwich was a major institution, one of the most important intellectual and cultural centres in medieval England. In the early fourteenth century it was undergoing something of a renaissance; it must have been an exciting time for both the ordinary monks and the monastic officials. A substantial building programme was in progress, partly as a result of a riot and subsequent fire in 1272 which had destroyed many of the Cathedral buildings. By 1300 the spire had been repaired and a new cloister, with an extensive programme of imagery, was beginning to rise on the south side of the church. A new stone belfry featuring a magnificent astrological clock was installed in 1322–25, one of the earliest in Britain, with a sun and moon, and numerous automata, including a choir of monks.[57] The monastery also had a considerable library, containing four to five hundred works by 1325. Most of these were text books, given by monks who had bought them for their own use while at university and later passed them on to

59 Ormesby Psalter, January page of Calendar, showing detail of shelfmarks. Oxford, Bodleian Library MS. Douce 366, fol. 2r.

their home institutions. None can be associated with Robert of Ormesby, but one W. de Ormesby, possibly Robert's brother, donated a very handsome set of late-thirteenth-century volumes of the glossed Bible.[58]

If Robert was himself subprior he must have taken great pleasure in using the manuscript which he himself had donated during the performance of the Divine Office in the cathedral. He seems to have remained at Norwich for almost all the rest of his life, making a final appearance in the records in 1350 when, along with a number of others, he was granted a passport to go abroad as a pilgrim. He may well have been over 70 by this time, but his family was perhaps in general long-lived. His brother John was at least 68 when he died in 1350. Even for an elderly monk, the arrival of the plague in Norwich in 1349 must have provided a strong incentive for departure. Of the sixty-four to sixty-seven monks at Norwich on the eve of the Black Death thirty succumbed, and the bishop's palace next to the Cathedral was described as being made almost intolerable by the stench of the dead. Whether Robert managed to take advantage of his pilgrim status and escaped abroad, or perished with so many others of his brethren, we cannot know. If he did stay, one can only hope his marvellous manuscript offered some comfort in such terrible times.

The Earl of Ufford and the final campaign

Even after Robert's death or departure, work on the Psalter was not over. Although it was bound, and therefore usable, on some pages the illumination was only partially executed and on many there was no illumination at all. Medieval manuscripts were sometimes left with decoration unfinished and perhaps this would also have been the case with the Ormesby Psalter had not events at Norwich overtaken it. At some time after January 1340, however, there was a final campaign of work on the manuscript, including rebinding, painting of the fore-edges, and possibly finishing off of the initials. What motivated Norwich to undertake this last phase?

We know that the current binding of the Ormesby Psalter is not its original binding from the unused sewing holes visible in the spines of some of the quires and from the unusual

60 The painted fore-edges of the Ormesby Psalter, after 1340. Oxford, Bodleian Library MS. Douce 366.

arrangement of the sewing bands visible inside the back cover. Moreover, the back boards have been split and repaired by iron bands, and the Calendar and the edges of some other folios show signs of what seems to be water damage. A large damp stain runs down the outer edge of each folio in the Calendar and damp has warped the parchment, causing vertical creases, which run the whole length of the leaves. The quires seem to have been ironed and scraped after exposure to damp. The lower margin of each quire is worn thin and marked by deep creases, and the leaves were perhaps clipped or pasted together to stretch out the warping: there are marks of clips at both top and bottom of the outer margins, and circular yellow marks on the outer edges of some folios. Did some accident befall the manuscript to account for this rebinding and repair?

On 15 January 1362 a violent storm shook the city of Norwich, toppling the cathedral's wooden spire and sending it crashing through the roof of the east end of the church. The choir stalls at Norwich had seats for seventy monks, with special places allotted to the most important officials. The stall of the subprior, to which Robert had assigned the manuscript, was the second return stall on the north side, and would have been directly under the collapsing spire. The book was presumably closed, and the boards of the binding were doubtless split by falling masonry, while water damaged the first quire and the edges of other folios.

Once the book had been rescued from the rubble, the cathedral seized the opportunity and set about both restoring and improving it. It was disbound and trimmed, slicing off the edges of the decoration on fols 9v and 38r. The soaked and damaged Calendar was removed and repaired, and the dedica-tion inscription copied out by a professional scribe in a more prominent position facing the opening of the Calendar. The spaces for initials were filled in a uniform and mediocre style by an artist aptly dubbed by Sydney Cockerell 'the Cheap Finisher'. It was then rebound in its current binding, using the broken boards for the back cover rather than the front.

As part of this final campaign, the fore-edges were painted with seven emblazoned shields nestling in a background of twining foliage (FIGURE 60). These are a remarkable survival of what was once an important part of the decoration of many medieval manuscripts. Later rebinding and trimming have destroyed the vast majority of such decorated fore-edges, although they appear quite often in fourteenth- and fifteenth-century pictures of saints and apostles holding books. Although now faded, the fore-edges of the Ormesby Psalter were originally brilliantly coloured: the vegetation was green and orange, the shields surrounded with red, blue and bright green

61 Chemise binding of the Ormesby Psalter, here shown open at fols 64v–65r. Oxford, Bodleian Library MS. Douce 366.

lobes – perhaps intended as flower petals, floral designs being popular for fore-edges – and traces of gold can be seen among the stems.

Three of the coats of arms on these shields are unremarkable. The English royal arms are shown in the quartering introduced in 1340, and are accompanied by the arms of the See of Norwich and those of the Cathedral Priory. The fourth shield requires some explanation. The arms of Robert de Ufford, Earl of Suffolk (1298–1369), appear on both the upper and the lower edges. Robert was one of the great men of the age. Not only a major local magnate, with extensive holdings across Norfolk, he was also one of Edward III's most trusted warriors, councillors and diplomats. His arms were formerly found in the medieval windows of the nave of Norwich Cathedral, along with those of other local aristocracy, representing a roll-call of those who supported the monastery in some way. Did Sir Robert, a generous patron of the arts, contribute to the repair and rebinding of the Psalter after it was damaged, and take the opportunity to add his arms to the fore-edges?

Conclusion

To summarize, the Ormesby Psalter was executed in four distinct campaigns. It was begun in the late thirteenth century, perhaps for a highly placed ecclesiastic of whom nothing more is known, but the illumination was interrupted with but a small part complete. The majority of the decoration was completed during a second campaign associated with the Foliot and Bardolf families and via them with John de Warenne, Earl of Surrey. This took place in the 1310s, probably between 1316 and 1318–19 when John de Warenne was guardian of the young Richard Foliot. After this, the manuscript was abandoned again, and then taken up by Robert of Ormesby, subprior of Norwich Cathedral Priory in the 1330s. Robert had the manuscript adapted for use at Norwich, bound and donated it to Norwich Cathedral. A final campaign took place in the 1360s, when the manuscript was rebound and the fore-edges painted.

The division of labour and the number of different hands found in the manuscript are indicative of a complex network of artists situated in a single location. This accords with the picture of a number of small, perhaps family-run, workshops able either to work alone or to collaborate on larger projects on an ad hoc basis. Patrons could have returned to these shops over several decades, either commissioning new manuscripts or bringing books back to be updated. Later East Anglian books betray a knowledge of the Ormesby Psalter's illumination best accounted for by production within a continuous workshop tradition. Given the strong Norwich connections of many of the East Anglian manuscripts, and the Ormesby Psalter in particular, Norwich seems the most likely contender for the location of these workshops. It was the seat of an important diocese, and the second largest city in fourteenth-century England, with a population of 25,000 by 1333. Five illuminators are recorded as practising in the city between 1320 and 1339.[59]

John de Warenne, however, could call upon wider resources. The style of two of the illuminators, including the most celebrated artist of the manuscript, is closely related to that of the manuscripts illuminated for his wife's uncle, Renaud de Bar, Bishop of Metz. Could Messin artists either have been brought or travelled independently from Metz on the death of their former patron, and established themselves in Norwich? Scribes and illuminators were among the most mobile of medieval craftsmen, and Norwich, with its extensive international trade, is widely acknowledged to have been highly receptive to artistic influences from the Continent. In the 1330s the Bohun Earls of Hereford imported a Flemish illuminator to work on their manuscripts.[60] Not only would such a foreign import account for the difference scholars have perceived between the style of the Ormesby Psalter and that of mainstream East Anglian manuscripts centred around the Gorleston Psalter, but it would cast a new light on the importance of pan-European personal and family connections as a source of patronage and motivation for apparent shifts of style from one region to another. The Ormesby Psalter sits at the heart of a geographical spider's web of artistic and aristocratic channels spreading both over East Anglia and across northern Europe, a web which it is hoped will richly repay further investigation.

INTRODUCTION   101

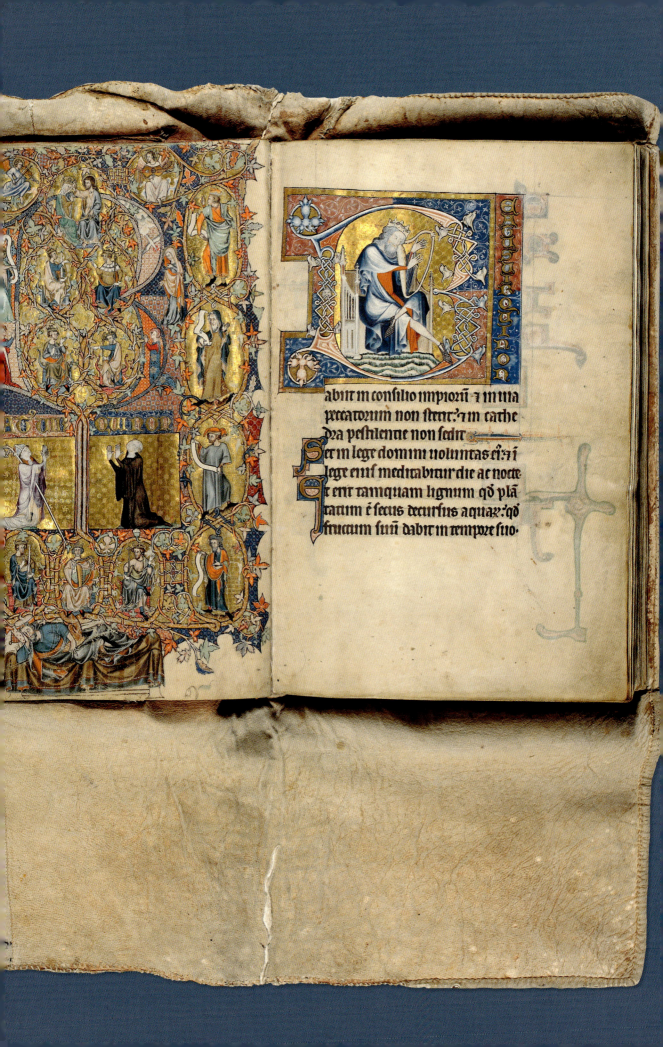

THE ORMESBY PSALTER

DESCRIPTIVE COMMENTARY

I

Psalm 1, *Beatus vir*

fol. 9v

Psalm 1 has two large *Beatus* initials facing each other across a single opening. On the left is a Jesse Tree, one of the traditional themes for the first psalm, painted in the 1310s on a single leaf and eventually tipped into the manuscript facing the page it was meant to replace. The image of a populated tree depicting the genealogy of Christ served to connect the Old and New Testaments, linking the psalms' supposed author, David, with their supposed subject, Christ. The concept of the Jesse Tree was derived from Isaiah's prophecies of the virgin birth (Isaiah 7:14, 'Behold a virgin shall conceive and bear a son, and his name shall be called Emmanuel', and 11:1–3, combined with the genealogy of Christ in the Gospel of Matthew (1.1–17).

At the bottom of the page Jesse reclines asleep, the trunk growing from his loins. Above him the kings of Judah and the prophets who predicted Christ's birth perch in the interlaced branches of the tree. At the top is the Annunciation, with Gabriel standing in the upright of the B and gesturing across the letter to Mary, who simultaneously turns away and looks back over her shoulder in awed acceptance of God's will. Above her the Holy Ghost flies down from Heaven to inseminate her through her ear. At the top of the Tree the upper boughs entwine around a pair of musical angels who accompany the Coronation of the Virgin.

Devotion to the Virgin was widespread in medieval Europe, and both Latin and vernacular religious lyrics repeatedly stress her multiple roles as virgin, mother, queen of Heaven, fulfil-ment of biblical prophecies and intercessor for sinful mankind. She often featured prominently in Jesse Trees, both as Christ's mother and from the medieval word-play on *virga* and *virgo* (rod and Virgin). Here the Virgin turns to her Son, her hands clasped in prayer as he places the Crown of Heaven on her head. Her gesture is imitated by two small figures dressed in heraldic robes

COMMENTARY 105

bearing the arms of the Foliot and Bardolf families, who gaze up at her from the base of the initial.

Heraldic decoration suggests that this phase of work on the Psalter was commissioned by John de Warenne, Earl of Surrey, to commemorate the betrothal of his ward, Richard Foliot, with an unidentified Bardolf girl. The combination of Annunciation and Coronation would have been especially appropriate in a psalter intended to mark a betrothal. There was a strong liturgical association between the Annunciation, bridal imagery and crowning in the Middle Ages, and the coronation of the bride formed a part of the marriage ceremony. The Virgin was regarded as a particularly suitable role model for women, and her dual portrayal as both bride and mother would have been a proper focus for the devotion of the young Bardolf bride, whose primary validation would have been achieved through marriage and motherhood. The sacred genealogy of Christ would also have recalled the importance of dynastic succession in this world. Their precarious dynastic situation must have been a great concern to the Foliots after the death of Richard, 2nd Lord Foliot, before March 1317, leaving two small daughters and a son who can have been no more than 5.

The figures of the monk and the bishop kneeling below the opening words of the psalm belong to a later campaign which also produced the large initial of King David on the opposite page. They were painted over the first verses of the psalm, and the black ink of the letters is partially visible through their garments. The monk can be identified as Robert of Ormesby, who adapted the manuscript and presented it to Norwich Cathedral Priory where he was subprior in the 1330s. The bishop could be Thomas of Hemenhale, in whose election in 1336/7 Robert was involved.

2

Psalm 1, *Beatus vir*

fol. 10r

The large initial above the psalm text shows King David, the supposed author of the Psalms, crowned and richly dressed, seated cross-legged on a Gothic throne. David, the eighth son of Jesse, lived about one thousand years before Christ. He was descended from the tribe of Judah and succeeded Saul, the first king of Israel. In the Middle Ages he was regarded as a 'type' or forerunner of Christ, and his triumph over Goliath was seen as prefiguring Christ's victory over Satan. David began life as a shepherd boy, and joined Saul's entourage as a musician. An image of him harping appears at the beginning of many psalters from the twelfth century onwards, usually in the guise of an aged enthroned king. His stance was typical of rulers in medieval art and had connotations of power and authority.

abiit in consilio impiorū ⁊ in uia
peccatorum non stetit: ⁊ in cathe
dra pestilentie non sedit.
Set in lege domini uoluntas eī: ⁊ in
lege eius meditabitur die ac nocte
Et erit tamquam lignum q̄d plā
tatum ē secus decursus aquaꝝ: q̄d
fructum suū dabit in tempore suo.

3

Psalm 26, *Dominus illuminatio mea*

fol. 38r

The Anointing of David was one of the conventional English subjects for Psalm 26. The episode is described in the first Book of Kings, which tells how the Lord sent the prophet Samuel to Bethlehem to anoint a new king from among the sons of Jesse. All Jesse's sons were rejected in turn until eventually the youngest, who was busy minding the sheep, was sent for and anointed with oil by the prophet. In the Ormesby initial, Samuel, dressed in a pale blue cloak, inverts a horn over the head of the kneeling David. Above, God descends from Heaven, carrying a blue shield emblazoned with a gold cross, illustrating his defence of the psalmist described in the first verse of the psalm, 'The Lord is my light and protection, of whom shall I be afraid?' To the right five mailed knights peer out from a walled city with a tower, battlements and a portcullis, in response to the third verse, 'If armies in camp should stand together against me, my heart will not fear.'

Watching from the upright of the initial is a knight in armour leaning on a long spear. This figure has sometimes been interpreted as the giant Goliath, whom David defeated shortly after his Anointing. However, his position, removed from the action of the initial, the rich materials used for his dress and the care taken to show the latest technological advances in his armour (he wears hinged greaves on his legs and his bascinet has a moveable visor) suggest a contemporary rather than a biblical figure. He originally bore the Foliot arms on his shield and tunic, and the words of the psalm should perhaps be understood as referring directly to him. The status of baronial families like the Foliots was intimately bound up with their right and duty to bear arms, and this psalm, with its cry of encouragement to the beleaguered warrior, must have had resonance for them. The elder Richard Foliot died campaigning in Scotland, possibly at Bannockburn in 1314, alongside one of his feudal overlords, Gilbert de Clare.

am tuam famulis tuis suppliciter: 7 fac
nos in tua ueritate deuotos. ut actib; nostris
 innocentia restitutis: liberari mereamur
ab impiis. per

ominus illuminatio
mea et salus mea: quem
timebo.

Dns ptector uite mee:
a quo trepidabo

Dum appropiant super me nocentes: ut e
dant carnes meas.

Qui tribulant me inimici mei: ipsi infir
mati sunt 7 ceciderunt.

Si consistant aduersum me castra: non ti
mebit cor meum.

Si exurgat aduersum me prelium: in hoc
ego sperabo.

Unam petii a domino hanc requiram: ut i

Adjacent to the top corner the initial line ending shows the arms of the Earl of Warenne, positioned directly above the word *dominus* (lord). The earls of Warenne were feudal overlords of the Foliot family at their main seat at Gressenhall, and John de Warenne, the seventh earl, was guardian of the younger Richard Foliot in the period in which the Psalter was illuminated.

The border is inhabited by a range of lively animals, birds and *babewyns*. A large hawk tears at a drumstick, an owl rotates its head backwards to gaze at a magpie, and a robin and goldfinch confront each other on either side of the lateral border. Alongside them are creatures from the realm of the absurd. In the upper border, two grotesques attack a giant snail and a butterfly. In the lower a cockerel with a man's torso creeps up behind an unwary squirrel eating a nut.

The meaning of such marginal motifs has been widely debated. Do they reflect an increasing appreciation of the natural world or were they intended to ward off evil? Are they manifestations of the psychological state of the artist, or bearers of some deeper moral or theological significance? Are they visual puns on words in the text, intended as mnemonics to aid the recollection of the psalms? Dragons were often understood as symbols of the Devil, while the goldfinch represented Christ's Passion, and the owl – with its daylight blindness and propensity to inhabit graveyards – stood for the Jews. Hawks were sporting birds, but Christ was also described in English lyrics as winning sinners to grace by showing his wounds, as a falconer lures back his hawk by offering it meat.

While some of these images perhaps had a now-lost significance for a visually literate medieval audience, records and surviving fragments show that similar pictures appeared in purely decorative contexts, on floor tiles, tableware and bed hangings. Even in liturgical manuscripts, the primary function of the fantastic and naturalistic creatures in the borders was surely to intrigue and delight the viewer, then as now.

4

Psalm 38, *Dixi custodiam vias meas*

fol. 55v

Both initial and border are by the Ormesby Master, and were executed in the 1310s as part of the second campaign of work on the manuscript. The initial shows the trial of Christ as described by John (18:28–40), an unusual but strikingly apt subject for a psalm whose theme is the patience of the just man in the face of accusation. Pilate and Christ are surrounded by a motley crew, some caricatured to emphasize their difference from the Psalter's aristocratic patrons. Two tall, richly dressed Jews with exaggerated physiognomies stand between Christ and Pilate. Behind them are their servants, one with close-cropped curly hair and African features. Pilate himself is depicted in a Jewish hat and with a distorted Jewish physiognomy, reflecting a moral judgement on his responsibility for the Crucifixion.

A variety of likely and unlikely beings perch in the border around the text. Next to the initial an elegant lady picks flowers, typical of the courtly activities often shown in the margins of Gothic manuscripts. Above her a dog-headed *babewyn* in women's dress looks across at her male counterpart in the opposite border. Christ was described by medieval exegetes as being led to his Trial by dogs, and the raised hand on the end of the female's tail parodies the gestures of the leading accuser in the initial. The male is biting or licking an acorn, perhaps inspired by references to tongues and mouths in the text next to him.

The main action takes place in the lower border, which shows the Hunt of the Unicorn. According to the bestiary, the unicorn is so fierce that is can only be captured by means of a trick. A virgin is left alone in the forest, and as soon as the unicorn sees her it springs into her lap. This story was interpreted as an allegory of the Incarnation, when Christ descended into the womb of the Virgin Mary. The positioning of the imagery here,

te deploramus: valeamus evincere in
sultationes aduersantium vittorū. Pex
it custodiam vias
meas: ut non delin
quam in lingua me
a. Posui ori meo cu
stodiam: cum con
sisteret aduersum me.
Obmutui 7 humiliatus sum 7 silui a bo
nis: 7 dolor meus renouatus est
Concaluit cor meum intra me: 7 in me
ditatione mea exardescet ignis.
Locutus sum in lingua mea: notū fac
michi domine finem meum.
Et numerum dierum meorum qui est:
ut sciam quid desit michi.
Ecce mensurabiles posuisti dies meos:
7 substantia mea tamqm nichilū ante te

however, shows an awareness of another level of symbolism expounded by the thirteenth-century bestiary of Guillaume le Clerc:

> This wonderful beast
> Which has one horn on its head
> Signifies our Lord
> Jesus Christ our Saviour.
> He is the spiritual Unicorn
> Who took up in the Virgin his abode
> Who is so especially worthy.
> His people of the Jews
> Believed him not, but spied on him
> And then took him and bound him.
> Before Pilate they led him
> And there condemned him to death.

The border scene acts as an analogy for the Trial in the initial, a metaphorical link emphasized by the prominent wound in the unicorn's side, reminiscent of Christ's wounding at the Crucifixion. The composition of the marginal vignette is very close to the scene of the hunt of the unicorn in the bestiary of Renaud de Bar, down to the ambivalent gesture of the lady and the stance of the hunter with his long spear. Typically, the Ormesby Master has undermined the seriousness of the analogy by the mocking gaze of the 'push-me, pull-you' *babewyn* in the corner, which sports a startling green hook-nosed face in place of his rear.

COMMENTARY 115

q̄s in uiscerib; nr̄is spm̄ scm̄ tuum quo
laudem tuam annuntiare possimus; ut
uero principalig; spu confirmari mera
mur eternis sedib; in ier̄l̄m celeste 2 pōnp
uid gloriaris in ma-
licia; qui potens es in
iniquitate.
Tota die iniusticiam
cogitauit lingua tua:
sicut nouacula acuta fecisti dolum.
Dilexisti maliciam super benignitatem:
iniquitatem magis quam loqui eq
uitatem.
Dilexisti omnia uerba precipitationis:
lingua dolosa.
Propterea deus destruet te in finem euel
let te 7 emigrabit te de tabernaculo tu
o; 7 radicem tuam de terra uiuentium.

5

Psalm 51, *Quid gloriaris in malitia*

fol. 71v

In this initial the Ormesby Master has depicted the murder of the priests of Nob, one of the traditional subjects for this psalm. The episode is recounted in 1 Kings 22:9–19. Doeg the Edomite reported to Saul that the priest Ahimelech had aided David in his flight from Saul, so the king sent Doeg to kill Ahimelech and the other priests. Psalm 51 was thought to have been composed by David in condemnation of Doeg's actions.

Next to the initial is the mildly scatological image of a dog-headed *babewyn* sniffing the naked bottom of a pot-bellied man who reaches up to grasp the body of a dragon which he seems to be swallowing. A delight in bawdy humour was a trait of both arts and literature of the Middle Ages and exposure of the buttocks was seen as a gesture of defiance and contempt. Sniffing bottoms is a particularly canine trait, but here the motif acts as a derogatory visual commentary on Doeg and his accomplices. The partially humanized face of the *babewyn* and the sword grasped in its tail recall the face and sword of one of the assassins in the adjoining initial, an inventive insult perhaps stimulated by the similarity between the name 'Doeg' and the word 'dog'.

In the lower border is an episode from the popular tales of the arch-thief and trickster Reynard the Fox. An elegant fox escapes with a cock slung over one shoulder, pursued by an enraged housewife shouting and waving her distaff in the air. The fox's fraudulent reputation was established by the bestiary, which saw him as a type of the Devil, out to fool the unwary. Tales of the fox's cunning derived from the French *Roman de Renard* became widely known through their use in sermons as *exempla*, illustrative anecdotes designed to make some moral point. Many *exempla* narratives were transferred to the visual arts, including stories of the fox.

Reynard's encounter with Chanticleer was recounted in both the *Roman* and in Marie de France's fables. Reynard

COMMENTARY 117

comes across Chanticleer sitting on a dung hill in a farmyard. Flattering him about the beauty of his voice, he tricks the vain cockerel into shutting his eyes and crowing as loudly as possible. The fox promptly seizes the cock by the neck and makes off with him. The farmer's wife, emerging from the farmhouse, sees him escaping with her prize bird and sets off in hot pursuit. Although the story might seem to be primarily a caution against vanity and folly, which were the cause of the cockerel's downfall, the viciousness and deceitfulness of the fox also provide a barnyard counterpart for that of Doeg in the initial.

6

Psalm 52, *Dixit insipiens*

fol. 72r

The D initial contains the conventional Christological subject for this psalm, the Temptation of Christ. According to Luke 4:2–13, Christ passed forty days fasting in the desert, during which time the Devil came to him and tempted him. In the first temptation, at the bottom left of the initial, the Devil offers Christ a stone, and urges him to prove his divine parentage by turning it into bread. Christ holds up one hand, palm out, in rejection of the Devil's blandishments. In the other he holds a book, illustrating his response: 'It is written that man liveth not by bread alone, but by every word of God'. The second and third temptations have been reversed for the sake of a better composition. At the top of the D, in the third temptation, Christ is shown seated on the pinnacle of the Temple of Jerusalem. The Devil hovers in the air beside him, one hand pointing to the ground where he urges Christ to throw himself. In the smaller initial T immediately above, two angels plunge headlong from Heaven, arms out-stretched, in response to the Devil's taunt that God's angels will protect him, 'lest perhaps thou dash thy foot against a stone'.

On the right, Christ is seated on a mound representing the high mountain to which the Devil led him for the second temp-tation. Below his feet is a pile of treasure, the material symbol of all the kingdoms of the world, which the Devil offers if Christ will kneel and adore him. He looks down on the fleeing Devil, who escapes out of the bottom of the initial.

Although this subject was widely used for Psalm 52 up to the mid-thirteenth century, from then on it was increasingly replaced by an illustration of King David debating with the Fool. By reverting to the traditional iconography the Ormesby Master has illustrated not only Psalm 52, only half a line of which appears on this page, but also the collect to Psalm 51, the theme of which is the rejection of the vanities of the world that comprise the Devil's second offer.

COMMENTARY 119

He returns, however, to the theme of the Fool in the lower margin. Here is a version of a widely known riddle in which a king challenges a low-born but clever opponent to come before him 'neither driving nor walking nor riding, neither dressed nor naked, neither out of the road nor in the road and bringing something that is a gift but no gift'. To the left the king emerges from a tower, accompanied by an attendant holding the leashes of two hounds, while on the right he is seated in debate with a young man.

Various solutions to this riddle appeared in manuscripts and misericords. Here, the story is combined with one of the many tales of the medieval anti-hero Marcolf. In the Latin 'Dialogue of King Solomon and Marcolf', Marcolf caps each of Solomon's proverbs with an earthy one of his own. Appended to the Dialogue were a series of tales in which the wily peasant repeatedly outwitted the wise king, in one of which Solomon banishes Marcolf from court, threatening to set the dogs on him if he returns. Marcolf does return and the threat is duly carried out, but he diverts the dogs by releasing a hare he has concealed under his clothes.

Here Marcolf, dressed only in a cape and one shoe, rides a goat and proffers a rabbit, which will escape as soon as it is released. The marginal riddle with the unholy fool outwitting the biblical wise man acts as a comic commentary on the debate of Christ and the Devil in the sanctified space of the initial.

7

Psalm 68, *Salvum me fac deus*

fol. 89r

In the initial for Psalm 68 the Ormesby Master has depicted the story of Jonah, a conventional subject inspired by the watery theme of the verse, 'Save me O Lord for the waters are come in to my soul'. According to the Old Testament account, Jonah was most reluctant to follow God's instructions to go and preach in the notoriously wicked city of Nineveh, and instead attempted to flee by ship to Tharsus (Jonah 1:3–2:11). The Lord sent a great tempest, and the mariners, in fear for their lives, cast lots to discover who was the cause of the storm. The lot fell on Jonah, who, accepting his fate, advised the sailors to cast him overboard. The moment they did so the storm abated. God caused Jonah to be swallowed by a great fish, in whose belly the prophet spent the next three days and nights before he was vomited up onto dry land.

In a parallel to the decoration of Psalm 51, the lower border here shows another test of resourcefulness solved by a clever peasant. An elderly man carries a bunch of greenery over one shoulder, and leads a wolf and a sheep towards a small boat. In the folk tale the man faces the problem of how to cross the river in a boat which will hold only himself and one other object without either the wolf eating the sheep or the sheep eating the greenery. He does it by taking the sheep over first, then on the second trip transporting the wolf over and bringing back the sheep. He crosses with the vegetation and finally returns to fetch the sheep.

In the upper border a fox leaning on crutches addresses a seated hare. In the literary version of this variant on the tales of Reynard the Fox, the gullible Chanticleer meets the fox disguised as a holy man and, taken in by his apparent piety, relaxes his guard and is immediately seized. The fox as a religious hypocrite, his deceitfulness hidden by his habit, appears widely in medieval misericords and in the margins

tuam intelligere teq; triumphatorem
mortis. sedentem ad patris dexteram
confiteri. per:

Saluum me fac deus:
qm intrauerunt aq
usq; ad aiam meam.
Infixus sum in li-
mo profundi: 7 non
est substantia.
eni in altitudinem maris: 7 tempestas
demersit me.
aboraui clamans rauce facte sunt:
fauces mee: defecerunt oculi mei dum
spero in deum meum.
ultiplicati sunt super capillos capitis
mei: qui oderunt me gratis
onfortati sunt qui persecuti sunt me
inimici mei iniuste: que non rapui

of manuscripts, sometimes in a pointed satire on the clergy: in the Gorleston Psalter and in a misericord at Ely Cathedral a fox dressed as a bishop preaches to a group of domestic fowl.

8

Psalm 80, *Exultate Deo*

fol. 109r

The opening verses of Psalm 80 contain an invitation to a musical feast:

> Rejoice to God our helper: sing aloud to the God of Jacob.
> Take a psalm, and bring hither the timbrel: the pleasant psaltery
>   with the harp.
> Blow up the trumpet on the new moon.

Most Gothic psalters contain a literal illustration of King David as a musician for this psalm, and the Ormesby Psalter is no exception. The artist had paid particularly close attention to the text, however. In the upper half of the E David plays a series of bells, representing the timbrel mentioned in the psalm, while his accompanists have a long horn and a harp, the trumpet and psaltery.

In the lower border two men dressed only in the loose braies worn by labourers engage in a wrestling match. Wrestling was a popular sport in the Middle Ages and was frequently illustrated in the margins of manuscripts and on misericords. Here the contestants grasp at lengths of cloth twisted around each other's shoulders. Similar contests were depicted in the margins of the Gorleston and Luttrell Psalters and on misericords at Hereford, Gloucester and Ludlow. The large grotesque that watches and waves a finger at the match is perhaps a parody of the referee who appears in the Ludlow version, his asses' ears a derogatory reflection on his intelligence.

While on one level scenes of games and sports such as this reflected the everyday activities of medieval life, in the margins of devotional texts they can take on other connotations. The wrestlers here act as a subtle allusion to the traditional English subject for this initial, Jacob wrestling the angel. As at Psalm 51, the artist plays with the different conventions of psalter illustration, using the unsanctified space of the border to show burlesque counterparts to the sacred histories in the initials.

The struggle of the wrestlers is parodied by the battle of two *babewyns* in the upper border. A young woman with a quadruped body uses a cooking pot and spoon to ward off the attack of a hooded male biped armed with a scimitar and mask-like shield. Battles of the sexes form a significant theme in the minor arts of the Middle Ages. The collapse of male authority and the triumph of women were seen as part of the upside-down world of the *monde renversée*, which is also inhabited by the young man in the right-hand border who drops his sword in horror at the sight of a gigantic snail. Combat between a man and a snail was a frequently recurring motif in the margins of Gothic manuscripts, and has been interpreted in various ways, from having sexual connotations to being an indictment of a particular ethnic group, the Lombards, who had a reputation for being turncoats. Most immediately, the snail hiding in its shell was regarded as a symbol of illusory courage, and flight before such a harmless creature was a satire on cowardice.

9

Psalm 97, *Cantate domino*

fol. 128r

As in the majority of English Gothic psalters, the initial for Psalm 97 contains a literal illustration of the opening line of the psalm, 'Sing unto the Lord a new song'. The Ormesby Master has depicted a group of tonsured monks in mass vestments gathered around an elegant lectern. Behind the lectern, a young novice in a monkish habit waits to turn the page, and above Christ leans down from a cloud to listen.

In the lower border a knight in armour vigorously decapitates a multi-headed dragon. His long sword points directly at the word *brachium* in the text above, and on one level the image acts as a visualization of the whole line: *Salvavit sibi dextera eius et brachium sanctum eius*, 'His right hand hath wrought for him salvation and his arm is holy.' Seemingly secular imagery of armed conflict had been used since the twelfth century as a metaphor for one of the Psalms' main themes; the constant battle against the forces of evil, which stood at the heart of Christian life. Knights could act as an image of Christ himself, the armoured *Christus miles*, while dragons were a common symbol of the Devil. Red multi-headed dragons immediately recall the Satanic creature of the Book of Revelation.

The knight here bears on his shield and epaulettes the arms of the Foliot family, for whom armed conflict against the forces of chaos must have had a particular resonance. Both Jordan, the first Lord Foliot, and his son Richard, respectively grandfather and father of the young Richard for whom the Psalter was intended, had served the English kings' successive campaigns against the Scots, and the elder Richard had been killed there.

On another level, the vignette of the battle functions as an exposition of the initial scene of the monks singing the psalms. The concept of the monk as Christ's warrior lay at the heart of Benedictine Rule, which shaped the monastic and to some extent the lay spiritual experience of Western Europe. The

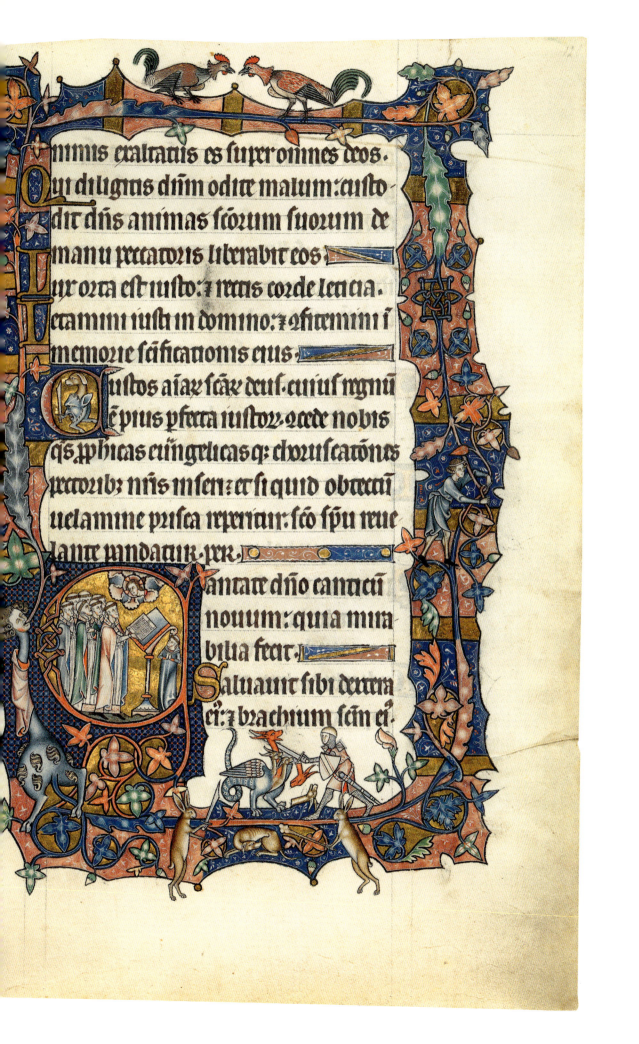

psalms themselves were regarded as powerful weapons in the continual war against the Devil, and their recitation was in itself an act of *bellum spirituale*, spiritual warfare.

Typically, the seemingly serious message of this page dissolves around the borders. Immediately below the knight and dragon, in bathetic mimicry of their battle, two hares attack a sleeping hound. The arming of animals with human weapons is typical of the Gothic *monde renversée*, and hares and rabbits attacking or hunting hounds were an especially popular reversal of the normal order. In the upper border is a cockfight, a popular medieval pastime, and widely depicted in the margins of Gothic manuscripts. Next to the initial, a bizarre long-necked biped opens his mouth to parody the singers in the initial, but only foliage emerges.

10

Psalm 101, *Domine exaudi orationem meam*

fol. 131r

The initial for Psalm 101 shows King David kneeling in prayer before Christ, who is seated on a band of cloud. He raises his right hand in blessing, promising a positive response to the psalmist's plea. Between David and Christ a scroll unfurls, on which the opening words of the psalm, 'O Lord hear my prayer', are inscribed. Next to the initial a young man plays a long, recorder-like instrument in a musical accompaniment to the psalm.

In the upper border a grotesque with an owl-like face confronts an elderly man, whose hands rest on crutches. His head and shoulders protrude from a snail's shell in a mocking parody of the slowness of the man who has lost the use of his legs. Physical deformity was often regarded as an outward sign of spiritual evil in the Middle Ages and cripples were thought to exaggerate or fake deformities to increase their income. Images of cripples might also have had an apotropaic function, warding off evil.

In the lower border a young man proffers or possibly receives a ring from an elegant woman. The two have all the trappings of the knightly class. A falcon perches on his wrist, while she holds a squirrel, a popular pet for aristocratic ladies. Between them sits a sedate hound, while below a large tabby cat is poised to spring upon a mouse peeping from a hole. This combination of the courtly couple and surrounding animals and grotesques has been interpreted as having sexual significance. The man's dagger has phallic overtones, while women and cats have been equated since classical times as insatiable sexual predators, with the mouse/man as prey. The term 'mousetrap' was even used as a euphemism for the female pudendum in one fifteenth-century English lyric. Hounds and hunting also frequently had erotic overtones, while the gaze of the watching grotesque, his face between his legs, adds a voyeuristic element.

COMMENTARY 131

This sexually charged imagery recalls Psalm 101's role as the first of the Penitential Psalms, composed by David in remorse for his adultery with Bathsheba. Medieval commentators interpreted the psalm as a whole as a commentary on the misery of the human condition brought about by the Fall of Man. Line 6, the last line on this page, was understood as referring to Eve's ready yielding to the Devil's blandishments, and subsequent persuasion of Adam to do the same. The blame for the expulsion from Paradise and the resulting miseries are placed firmly on the Beast-like lust which was a consequence of the weakness of the woman: 'Because they listened to the Devil they come together through lust in the manner of beasts; they brought forth in misery and groaning.' The seemingly courtly vignette of the lovers, with its surrounding animals and grotesques, acts as a warning reminder of the bestial nature of carnal passion.

11

Psalm 109 *Dixit dominus domino meo*

fol. 147v

Psalm 109 marks the last of the liturgical divisions of the psalms, and was the first psalm used in Sunday Vespers. Its initial is especially large and splendid. The D occupies ten lines of text and the opening words of the psalm are written in gilded display capitals in a vertical column beside the initial. These words, 'The Lord said unto my Lord: sit thou at my right hand', provide the cue for an illustration of the first two persons of the Trinity, here shown as identical enthroned figures with cruciform halos, hands raised in the *orans* gesture of prayer. Their setting and stance recall depictions of Christ at the Last Judgement, also occasionally shown at this psalm. The feet of the left-hand figure rest on a footstool beneath which crouch mailed soldiers in response to the second verse of the psalm, *Donec ponam inimicos tuos scabellum pedum tuorum*, 'Until I make thy enemies my footstool'. The third person of the Trinity is represented by another Christ-like head in the initial to the collect above. A pair of seraphim on golden wheels, their wings dotted with eyes, stand in the uprights of the initial, and four small birds perch around it. Small quick-flying birds were sometimes used to symbolize the soul of the Christian, who spiritually strives to fly to Heaven. Next to the initial, a naked trumpeter wrapped in a cloth twists away from us to blow a long trumpet over his shoulder.

In the upper border a monkey falconer accompanied by a running hound swings a lure for an owl seated backwards on a fleeing rabbit. This parody of hawking was perhaps triggered by the reference to pursuers in the top line of the text, just as the contorted figure in the left border below the initial acts out the sitting down referred to in the adjacent psalm verse.

The main action takes place in the lower border, where a dragon sticks its tongue out at a bizarre battle. A lion and a bear ridden by two nude men are locked in an intense combat.

COMMENTARY   135

The riders, whose appearance echoes that of their mounts, grab at each others' hair and faces. Lions and bears in combat appear in the margins of the Smithfield Decretals and in a late-fourteenth-century misericord at Norwich. According to the bestiary, the lion was the symbol of Christ while the bear was commended for its strength and its care for its young. Bears were also thought to be the animal closest to humanity, as they could stand upright and copulate face to face and lying down like people. Both animals could also have negative connotations, however, and in psalters David is sometimes shown defending his flocks from the lion and the bear.

The significance here is perhaps more immediately political. Both bears and lions could stand for particular places and people in late-thirteenth- and fourteenth-century England. The lion was strongly associated with the Plantagenet family and by extension with the kingdom of England as a whole, while the bear was used to denote Berwick and hence Scotland. In the 1330s Thomas Bradwardine, Oxford scholar and later Archbishop of Canterbury, used the image of a battle between these two animals as a way of recalling to mind the English victory over the Scots at Berwick. The ferocious battle in the border of Psalm 109 might have recalled for its viewers the seemingly endless struggles of England and Scotland, which cost the life of the father of the young man whose betrothal the manuscript was intended to celebrate.

APPENDIX

DESCRIPTION OF THE MANUSCRIPT

Provenance

- An unknown patron, possibly an East Anglian ecclesiastic (late-thirteenth-century campaign).
- Probably John de Warenne, Earl of Surrey and Sussex (d. 1347) to commemorate an unfulfilled engagement of *c.* 1314–19 between his ward, Richard Foliot (d.1325) and an unknown Bardolf girl. Donor figures bearing Foliot and Bardolf arms on fol. 9v and heraldic decoration throughout the manuscript.
- Robert of Ormesby, monk of Norwich Cathedral Priory and probably subprior in 1336/7. Inscription in red on 1v and erased inscription on fol. 8v.
- Norwich Cathedral Priory. Above inscriptions, Norwich press marks *A.I* and *xlij* on fol. 2r and arms of Norwich Cathedral Priory and the See of Norwich on fore-edges along with those of England adopted in 1340, and the Earl of Ufford.
- A. Gray, 1654. Signature and date on front flyleaf.
- Francis Douce (1757–1834). Bookplate on inside cover; acquired from Thomas Thorpe, bookseller, November 1831.
- Oxford, Bodleian Library, MS. Douce 366; bequest of Francis Douce, 1834.

Physical description

- 213 folios, parchment, approx. 377 mm × 253 mm, complete, 20 quires with catchwords up to fol. 201v.
- Collation: flyleaf, i⁸, 1 + ii¹², iii–xviii¹², xix¹⁰, xx⁴ (the last two forming the flyleaf and paste-down).
- 18 lines, ruled in lead point with double bounding lines, and lines for both head and foot of letters.

- Text block approx. 232 mm × 139 mm, script written in black ink in a Gothic liturgical hand, *textualis precissa*.
- In a medieval binding of oak boards covered in pink skin with a skin chemise measuring approx. 625 mm x 740 mm, once also dyed pink.

Contents

- Calendar for Norwich Cathedral and Paschal Table in blue, red and burnished gold (fols 2r–8r).
- Psalter and Canticles with Collects (fols 9r–205v).
- First Litany and two Collects (fols 206–209v).
- Added Norwich Litany and thirteen Collects (fols 209v–213).

Decoration

- fol. 9v, Psalm 1 *Beatus vir*, 1310s campaign. Large initial B with Tree of Jesse containing the Annunciation and Coronation of the Virgin and a full border of kings and prophets, tipped in the wrong way around and with figures of monk and bishop added in 1330s campaign.
- fol. 10r, Psalm 1 *Beatus vir*, 1330s Campaign. Large (10-line) initial B containing King David seated on a throne playing a harp.

Section 1, late-thirteenth-century campaign, fols 10r–21v

Two-line psalm and collect initials in burnished gold and rich colours. The collect initials in this section contain foliage and small dragons and grotesques. Single-line verse initials in burnished gold against pink and blue grounds with white foliage ornament touched with red. The line fillers contain burnished gold, red and blue penwork designs, including a hound pursuing a hare, fish, zoomorphs and decorative flourishing.

- fol. 10v, Psalm 2, *Quare fremuerunt gentes*. King David debating with four laymen.
- fol. 11v, Psalm 3, *Domine quid multiplicati sunt*. Christ rising from the tomb, holding a banner and turning to bless a kneeling figure whose hands are raised in prayer; this figure was originally intended to wear a crown but when painted and gilded the design was changed to a green hat.

- fol. 12r, Psalm 4, *Cum invocarem exaudivit me*. King David kneeling before an altar, above which the Hand of God emerges from a cloud and blesses him; in the lower border a grotesque stands on the spiral foliate extension of the initial and fires an arrow from a bow at a dog perched on top of the initial frame, which in turn gazes up at a rabbit on top of the initial for the preceding collect.
- fol. 13r, Psalm 5, *Verba mea auribus percipe domine*. King David standing, and pointing to his mouth.
- fol. 14r, Psalm 6, *Domine ne in furore tuo*. King David on one knee, hands raised in *orans* gesture of prayer.
- fol. 15r, Psalm 7, *Domine deus meus*. King David kneeling before an altar, his hands raised in prayer, gazing up at the Hand of God which emerges from a cloud to bless him.
- fol. 16r, Psalm 8, *Domine dominus noster*. A bearded standing figure holding a large disc representing the world in his left hand and pointing to it with his right; a small grotesque perches on the foliate extension of the initial and gazes up at another grotesque with the body of a bird, the head of a man and the antlers of a stag, which is perched on the extension of the initial of the collect for Psalm 7.
- fol. 17r, Psalm 9, *Confitebor tibi domine*. The Last Judgement. Christ seated in a mandorla displaying the Wounds of the Passion, around him two tiers of figures in prayer. A bird grotesque with a human head perches on top of the initial frame and looks up at a magpie, which returns his gaze from the top of the initial to the collect for Psalm 8.
- fol. 20r, Psalm 10, the Ascension, *In domino confido*. Only Christ's feet and the bottom of his robe are visible as he ascends out of the top of the initial, watched by the Apostles. The body of the initial is formed by the tail of a dragon with a knotted neck and the head of a bishop. A blue bird perches on the bishop's mitre and seems to put something into his mouth.
- fol. 20v, Psalm 11, *Salvum me fac*. In the lower bowl of the S King David gestures to and simultaneously turns away from three men, one of whom reaches out to him; above Christ blessing leaning from a cloud.
- fol. 21v, Psalm 12, *Usquequo Domine*. A kneeling layman with a beard and long hair, hands raised in prayer, between

Hand of God emerging from cloud on one side and head of Christ on the other.

Sections 2 & 3, 1310s campaign, fols 22r–45v

Two-line historiated psalm initials and decorated collect initials in burnished gold and colours with vegetal extensions from the finials. Whilst many of the collect initials in this section are purely decorative or contain grotesques, some contain or are accompanied in the margin by large figures, which I describe below. Single-line verse initials in burnished gold against pink and blue grounds with white foliage ornament, occasional lions, dragons, hares and hounds, touched with red. Line fillers are a mix of burnished gold, red and blue penwork designs and fully painted fish, birds, hares and hounds, zoomorphs and heraldic shields. Blue and red flourishing in the lower margin of fols 22r–24r.

- fol. 22r, Psalm 13, *Dixit insipiens*. A Fool with a bladder on a stick and a round flat loaf with a hole in it, looking at opening words of psalm.
- fol. 23r, Psalm 14, *Domine quis habitabit in tabernaculo tuo*. A tonsured man in a blue-grey habit knocks on a door with a round door knocker while inserting a large key into the keyhole.
- fol. 23v, Psalm 15, *Conserva me domine*. The Last Judgement. Christ seated on a cloud displaying the Wounds of the Passion, the dead rising from their tombs below. In the border beside the initial a grotesque trumpeter emerges from a snail's shell and blows a horn to announce the Second Coming.
- fol. 24r, Collect, *Conserva nos domine*. In the border beside the initial a young male grotesque plays the bellows with a pair of tongs.
- fol. 24v, Psalm 16, *Exaudi domine justitiam meam*. A seated ape turns his back to the text.
- fol. 25v, Psalm 17, *Diligam te domine fortitudo mea*. The suicide of Saul. To the right Saul falls on his sword, while behind him a man pulls his crown off his head.
- fol. 29r, Collect, *Firmamentum spei*. In the border a young centaur combs its hair and gazes in a hand mirror.

- fol. 29r, Psalm 18, *Caeli enarrant gloriam dei*. The Virgin and Child. The Virgin is seated with the Christ Child on her knee. One arm is around the Child, and in one hand she holds a flowering branch for which the Christ Child reaches out.
- fol. 30r, Psalm 19, *Exaudiat te dominus*. The Sacrifice of Isaac. Abraham stands and raises his sword in his left hand, looking up over his left shoulder for an angel which is not shown. With his right hand he grasps the head of Isaac, who kneels on an altar, hands clasped in prayer. The head of the ram that will form the eventual sacrifice peeps out from behind Abraham.
- fol. 31r, Psalm 20, *Domine in virtute tua*. A young beardless king kneels and raises his hands in prayer.
- fol. 32r, Psalm 21, *Deus deus meus*. The Crucifixion. Christ on the Cross, with Longinus thrusting a spear into Christ's side and pointing to his eyes.
- fol. 34r, Collect, *Caput misericordie deus*. Inside the initial a seated man playing a recorder.
- fol. 34r, Psalm 22, *Dominus regit me*. Two men, hands raised in prayer, walking towards the open door of a domed building.
- fol. 34v, Collect, *Rege nos*. In the lower border a large, young male grotesque in a hood gazing out plaintively at the viewer. Bodiless, he walks on hand crutches.
- fol. 35r, Psalm 23, *Domini est terra*. The Resurrection. Christ stepping out of the tomb, blood flowing from his wounds, holding a banner in one hand and raising the other in blessing.
- fol. 35v, Psalm 24, *Ad te domine levavi animam meam*. A bearded layman kneeling in prayer inside a Gothic arch with battlements above.
- fol. 37r, Collect, *Libera nos*. A very fine portrait head of a king wearing a gold circlet.
- fol. 37r, Psalm 25, *Iudica me domine*. A young bearded layman kneeling in prayer, threatened by a Hellmouth below him.
- fol. 37v, Collect, *Largire quaesumus domine*. The head of a bishop.
- fol. 38r, Psalm 26, *Dominus illuminatio mea*. Large (5-line) historiated initial of the Anointing of David, with full border containing animals, birds and insects.
- fol. 39r, Collect, *Defende nos*. A young woman playing a viol.

APPENDIX 141

- fol. 39r, Psalm 27, *Ad te domine clamabo*. The Betrayal. Judas embraces Christ, while to their left a strangely contorted figure grabs at him from behind.
- fol. 40r, Psalm 28, *Afferte domino filii dei*. A bearded man kneels before an altar and holds up a small white ram as an offering.
- fol. 41r, Collect, *Dona domine*. A fine grotesque with a balding, bearded head and the body of a fish.
- fol. 41r, Psalm 29, *Exaltabo te domine*. A bearded man in a Jewish cap asperging a small building.
- fol. 42r, Psalm 30, *In te domine speravi*. Christ kneeling in prayer on a green mound, the Holy Ghost flying down from a cloud above.
- fol. 44r, Psalm 31, *Beati quorum*. A young man kneels to confess his sins to a monk in a brown robe.
- fol. 45r, Psalm 32, *Exultate iusti in domino*. A young man in a short tunic playing a viol. In the border next to the initial, a young man in a long robe dancing and playing a pair of pipes.

Section 4, 1310s campaign and Cheap Finisher, fols 46r–57v

With the exception of fol. 55v and incomplete designs for borders at fols 46v, 48, 50, 51, 53v and 56v by the Ormesby Master, this section contains two-line collect and psalm initials and line endings in burnished gold, pink and blue by the Cheap Finisher.

- fol. 55v, Psalm 38, *Dixi custodiam vias meas*. Large (5-line) initial containing the Trial of Christ with full border extending from initial finials, the Hunt of the Unicorn in the *bas-de-page*.

Section 5, 1310s campaign, fols 58r–69v

Two-line psalm and collect initials in burnished gold and rich colours with vegetal extensions from the initial finials, many inhabited by hounds, hares, mermaids and so on. The collect initials in this section contain only foliage or grotesques. Single-line verse initials in burnished gold against pink and blue grounds with white foliage ornament touched with red. Line endings have animals, birds, fish and foliage designs and a wide range of heraldic shields.

- fol. 58v, Psalm 40, *Beatus qui intelligit*. King David kneeling in prayer to head of Christ emerging from a cloud. A tree below.
- fol. 59r, Psalm 41, *Quemadmodum desiderat cervus*. As the last.
- fol. 60v, Psalm 42, *Iudica me deus*. King David kneeling and gesturing to the head of Christ emerging from a cloud.
- fol. 61v, Psalm 43, *Deus auribus nostris*. King David debating with a man in a cap, watched by a third man, the Hand of God emerging from a cloud above.
- fol. 63r, Psalm 44, *Eructavit cor meum*. King David kneeling in prayer before an altar, the head of Christ emerging from a cloud above.
- fol. 64v, Psalm 45, *Deus noster refugium*. King David kneeling before an altar on which lies an open book. Christ looks down from a cloud. The two appear to be engaged in a heated debate, and gesture vigorously to each other. Beside the initial a mermaid plays a viol.
- fol. 65v, Psalm 46, *Omnes gentes plaudite manibus*. As for Psalm 44, except that a man in a hood kneels behind David.
- fol. 66r, Psalm 47, *Magnus dominus*. To the right Christ standing and regarding gesturing to a domed and battlemented building on the left representing the Heavenly Jerusalem.
- fol. 67r, Psalm 48, *Audite haec omnes gentes*. King David stands to the right and with one hand gestures up to the Hand of God which emerges from a cloud. With the other he points down towards two seated figures who listen to his words.
- fol. 68v, Psalm 49, *Deus deorum*. As no space was left for an initial at the beginning of the psalm, the subject, which is the same as for Psalms 40 and 41, has been transferred to the collect initial.

Section 6, 1310s campaign, fols 70r–81v

Two-line decorated psalm and collect initials in burnished gold and colours, while line fillers contain some zoomorphs and the arms of Clare.

- fol. 71v, Psalm 51, *Quid gloriaris in malitia*. Large (5-line) initial of the murder of the priests by Doeg; full border springing from initial finials with Reynard the Fox in the *bas-de-page*.

APPENDIX 143

- fol. 72r, Psalm 52, *Dixit insipiens in corde suo.* Large (5-line) initial of the Temptations of Christ; full border springing from the initial finials, with Solomon and Marcolf in the *bas-de-page.*

Sections 7–13, 1310s campaign and Cheap Finisher, fols 82r–153v

Two-line psalm and collect initials and line fillers in burnished gold against pink and blue grounds with white decoration by the Cheap Finisher, with the exception of the main pages by the Ormesby Master.

- fol. 89r, Psalm 68, *Salvum me fac deus.* Large (5-line) initial of Jonah and the Whale; full border springing from the initial finials with the riddle of the Wolf, the Lamb and the Cabbages in the *bas-de-page.*
- fol. 109r, Psalm 80, *Exultate deo adiutori nostro.* Large (5-line) initial of King David and musicians; full border springing from the initial finials with a wrestling match in the *bas-de-page.*
- fol. 128r, Psalm 97, *Cantate domino.* Large (5-line) initial of monks singing; full border springing from the initial finials, with a knight fighting a dragon in the *bas-de-page.*
- fol. 131r, Psalm 101, *Domine exaudi orationem meam.* Large (5-line) initial of David kneeling in prayer to Christ; full border springing from the initial finials, with a betrothal in the *bas-de-page.*
- fol. 147v, Psalm 109, *Dixit dominus domino meo.* Large (10-line) initial containing the Trinity; full border springing from the initial finials with a battle between a lion and a bear with nude riders in the *bas-de-page.*

Sections 14 & 17, 1310s campaign and Cheap Finisher, fols 154r–165v and fols 190r–201v

- One completed page (fol. 154r) with burnished gold verse initials on blue and pink grounds set against an orange bar border.

- Designs for other bar borders terminating in foliage tendrils, some partially painted, from fols 154v to 165v and for line fillers with Foliot and Bardolf heraldry.
- Two-line psalm and collect and single-line verse initials and line fillers in burnished gold against pink and blue grounds with white decoration by Cheap Finisher.

Sections 15, 16, 18 & 19, Cheap Finisher, fols 166r–189v & fols 202r–213v

- Two-line psalm and collect initials, single-line verse initials and line fillers in burnished gold against pink and blue grounds with white decoration by Cheap Finisher up to fol. 209r.
- From fol. 209v, the added Norwich Litany, 1330s campaign blue initials with red penwork decoration.

NOTES

1. *[P]salterium fratris Roberti de Ormesby monachi Norwyc[ensis] per eunde[m] assignatu[m] choro ecclesi[a]e sanct[a]e Trinitatis Norwyci ad iacendu[m] coram Supp[ri]ore qui pro tempore fuerit in p[er]petuum*, fol. 1v.
2. Oxford, Bodleian Library MS. Douce c.68, fol.19r.
3. *Illuminated Ornaments Selected from Manuscripts and Early Printed Books from the Sixth to the Seventeenth Centuries*, Drawn and Engraved by Henry Shaw, F.S.A. with Descriptions by Sir Frederic Madden, London, 1833, no. IX.
4. Gustav Freidrich Waagen, *Treasures of Art in Great Britain: Being an Account of the Chief Collections of Paintings, Drawings, Sculptures, Illuminated Manuscripts &c &c.*, vol. III, London, 1854, pp. 92–5.
5. A handwritten note dated 4 July 1884, pasted in the front of the Bodleian's annotated copy of the 1840 catalogue of Douce's manuscripts. The manuscripts remained in the Douce Museum until they were transferred to the New Bodleian in 1940.
6. E.W.B. Nicholson's revisions to Falconer Madan, *Summary Catalogue of Western Manuscripts in the Bodleian Library, Oxford*, vol. V, Oxford, 1905, pp. xxii–xxvii, no. 21941.
7. Sydney C. Cockerell, *The Gorleston Psalter: A Manuscript of the Beginning of the Fourteenth Century in the Library of C.W. Dyson Perrins*, London, 1907, p. 2.
8. S.C. Cockerell and M.R. James, *Two East Anglian Psalters at the Bodleian Library, Oxford*, Oxford, 1926.
9. See Lucy Freeman Sandler, *Gothic Manuscripts 1285–1385*, vol. 2: *Catalogue*, volume V in *A Survey of Manuscripts Illuminated in the British Isles*, gen. ed. J.J.G. Alexander, London, 1986, pp. 49–51, no. 43 with bibliography.
10. *Age of Chivalry: Art in Plantagenet England 1200–1400*, ed. Jonathan Alexander and Paul Binski, exhibition catalogue, Royal Academy of Arts, London, 1987, p. 454, no. 573.
11. London, British Library Additional MS 49622, see Sandler, *Gothic Manuscripts*, vol. 2, pp. 56–8, no. 50, and Margot M. Nishimura and David Nishimura, 'Rabbits, Warrens and Warenne: The Patronage of the Gorleston Psalter', in Kathryn A. Smith and Carol H. Krinsky, eds, *Tributes to Lucy Freeman Sandler: Studies in Illuminated Manuscripts*, London and Turnhout, 2007, pp. 205–17; London, British Library Stowe MS 12, see Sandler, *Gothic Manuscripts*, vol. 2, pp. 86–7, no. 79; Cambridge, Fitzwilliam Museum MS. 1–2005, see Stella Panayotova, *The Macclesfield Psalter*, Cambridge, 2008 with bibliography; Douai, Bibliothèque municipale MS 171, see Sandler, *Gothic Manuscripts*, vol. 2, pp. 115–17, no. 105, and Caroline Susan Hull, 'Abbot John, Vicar Thomas and M.R. James: The Early History of the Douai Psalter', in Lynda Dennison, ed., *The Legacy of M.R. James: Papers from the 1995*

Cambridge Symposium, Donington, 2001, pp. 118–27, and her *The Douai Psalter and Related Manuscripts*, Ph.D. dissertation, Yale University, 1994; London, British Library Yates Thompson MS 14, see Sandler, *Gothic Manuscripts*, vol. 2, pp. 113–15, no. 104.

12. Cockerell and James, *Two East Anglian Psalters*, p. 31.

13. The idea was first expressed in Otto Pächt, 'A Giottesque Episode in English Medieval Art', *Journal of the Warburg and Courtauld Institutes* 6, 1943, pp. 51–70, and has won general acceptance among scholars since. See Hull, 'Abbot John, Vicar Thomas and M.R. James, pp. 121–6; L. Dennison, 'The Technical Mastery of the Macclesfield Psalter: A Preliminary Stylistic Appraisal of the Illuminators and their Suggested Origin', *Transactions of the Cambridge Bibliographical Society*, vol. 13, no. 3, 2006, pp. 253–88; Panayotova, *The Macclesfield Psalter*, pp. 23–8. See also P. Binski and D. Park, 'A Ducciesque Episode at Ely: The Mural Decorations of Prior Crauden's Chapel', *England in the Fourteenth Century: Proceedings of the 1985 Harlaxton Symposium*, ed. W.M. Ormrod, Woodbridge, 1986, pp. 28–41.

14. Cockerell and James, *Two East Anglian Psalters*, p. 21.

15. On the angels in the reliquary chapel, see Paul Binski, 'The Ante-Reliquary Chapel Paintings in Norwich Cathedral: The Holy Blood, St Richard and All Saints', in Julian M. Luxford and M.A. Michael, eds, *Tributes to Nigel Morgan, Contexts of Medieval Art: Images, Objects and Ideas*, Turnhout, 2010, pp. 241–3. For the Saxlingham Nethergate glass, see www.cvma.ac.uk/publications/digital/norfolk/sites/saxlinghamnethergate/history.html (accessed 11 August 2015). For the Carrow Psalters (Baltimore, Walters Art Gallery MS W.34) and the Madrid Psalter (Biblioteca Nacional MS 6422), see Nigel Morgan, *Early Gothic Manuscripts*, vol. 2: *1250–85*, volume IV in *A Survey of Manuscripts Illuminated in the British Isles*, gen. ed. J.J.G. Alexander, London, 1986, pp. 88–91, nos 118 and 120.

16. Oxford, Bodleian Library MS. Auct.D.4.8. See Nigel Morgan, *Early Gothic Manuscripts*, vol. 1: *1190–1250*, volume IV in *A Survey of Manuscripts Illuminated in the British Isles*, pp. 123–4, no. 75.

17. Cambridge University Archives MS. Luard 7★ and Luard 11★; see Paul Binski and Patrick Zutshi with Stella Panayotova, *Western Illuminated Manuscripts: A Catalogue of the Collections in Cambridge University Library*, Cambridge, 2011, pp. 118–21, nos 126 and 128. See also M.A. Michael, 'Urban Production of Manuscript Books and the Role of the University Towns', in *The Cambridge History of the Book in Britain*, vol. II: *1100–1400*, ed. Nigel Morgan and Rodney M. Thomson, Cambridge, 2008, pp. 168–94, esp. p. 190.

18. On Psalter collects, see R.W. Pfaff, 'Psalter Collects as an Aid to the Classification of Psalters', *Studia Patristica*, vol. 18, no. 2, 1989–91, pp. 397–402.

19. New York, Public Library MS Spencer 26. See *The Splendor of the Word: Medieval and Renaissance Illuminated Manuscripts at the New York Public Library*, ed. Jonathan J.G. Alexander, James H. Marrow and Lucy Freeman Sandler, exhibition catalogue, New York and London, 2005, pp. 201–7, no. 41.

20. The gilding is flaking to reveal what appears to be tarnished silver underneath.

21. My interpretation of this phase differs somewhat from that of Cockerell, *The Gorleston Psalter*, p. 23, and Sandler, *Gothic Manuscripts*,

vol. 2, p. 50, in that I believe the decoration of section 5 (fols 58r–67v) was carried out as part of this campaign rather than an earlier one.

22. On the possible datings of the phases of work on the Cloister, see Eric Fernie, *An Architectural History of Norwich Cathedral,* Oxford, 1996, pp. 167–71; Francis Woodman, 'The Gothic Campaigns', in Ian Atherton, Eric Fernie et al., eds, *Norwich Cathedral: Church, City and Diocese 1096–1996,* London, 1996, pp. 165–8; Veronica Sekules, 'The Gothic Sculpture', in the same volume, pp. 199–202, and her 'Religious Politics and the Cloister Bosses of Norwich Cathedral', *The Medieval Cloister in England and Wales,* ed. Martin Henig and John McNeil, *Journal of the British Archaeological Association* 159, 2006, pp. 288–9.

23. See Binski, 'The Ante-Reliquary Chapel Paintings in Norwich Cathedral, pp. 246–8, for the dating of the Norwich chapel paintings.

24. Richard Marks, *The Medieval Stained Glass of Northamptonshire,* Summary Catalogue 4 of *Corpus Vitrearum Medii Aevi: Great Britain,* Oxford, 1998, pp. 126–41.

25. They held lands at Burton Latimer, Great Harrowden and Wilby in the late twelfth and early thirteenth centuries; see William Page, *The Victoria County History of Northamptonshire,* vol. 3, 1930, pp. 164–8, 180–86; vol. 4, 1937, pp. 178–85.

26. F. Law-Turner, 'The Ormesby Psalter and a Lost Midlands Jesse Window: Media Cross Fertilisation in the Early Fourteenth Century', *Vidimus* 52, June 2011, http://vidimus.org/issues/issue-52/feature (accessed 3 September 2014).

27. Oxford, Bodleian Library MS. Douce 131. See Sandler, *Gothic Manuscripts,* vol. 2, pp. 117–18, no. 106.

28. Jennifer Clare Ward, *The Estates of the Clare Family, 1066–1317,* Ph.D. dissertation, University of London, 1962, p. 320; http://qmro.qmul. ac.uk/jspui/handle/123456789/1579 (accessed 5 September 2014).

29. London, Lambeth Palace Library MS 233. See *Sandler,* Gothic Manuscripts, vol. 2, pp. 35–6, no. 30.

30. Paris, Bibliothèque nationale de France, MS latin 3114; see http:// gallica.bnf.fr/ark:/12148/btv1b525038815.r=latin+3114.langEN (accessed 3 September 2014).

31. Pächt, 'A Giottesque Episode', pp. 54–6; J.J.G Alexander, 'An English Illuminator's Work in Some Fourteenth-Century Italian Law Books at Durham', in *Medieval Art and Architecture at Durham Cathedral,* volume 3 of *British Archaeological Association Transactions for 1977,* Leeds, 1980, pp. 149–53, esp. p. 150.

32. Prague, Státní knihovna XXIII C 120; Cambridge, Fitzwilliam Museum MS. 298; London, British Library Yates Thompson MS 8; Verdun, Bibliothèque municipale MS. 107. The Ritual, formerly Metz, Bibliothèque municipale MS. 43, was destroyed by bombing on 31 August 1944 but is known from photographs. See Alison Stones, *Gothic Manuscripts 1260–1320,* in *A Survey of Manuscripts Illuminated in France,* Part 1, vol. 1, London and Turnhout, 2013, pp. 39–41, 71–2, and Part 2, vol. 1, London and Turnhout, 2014, pp. 21–88, IV: Province of Trier and Duchy of Lorraine, County of Bar, Metz and Verdun, especially nos 6 to 9 and 16a and b; and her 'Les Manuscrits de Renaud de Bar', in A.-O. Poilpré and M. Besseyre, eds, *Production Livresque et Commande Artistique: L'écrit et le livre peint en Lorraine, de Saint-Mihiel à Verdun (IXe–XVe siècles),* Actes du colloque de Saint-Mihiel, 25–26 October 2010, Turnhout, 2014, pp. 271–312 (my thanks to Alison

Stones for sharing with me the proofs of this article and an invaluable discussion of the possible Metz–Ormesby links).

33. www1.arkhenum.fr/bm_verdun_ms/_app (accessed 12 August 2015).

34. Patrick M. de Winter, 'Une réalisation exceptionnelle d'enlumineurs français et anglais vers 1300: le bréviaire de Renaud de Bar, évêque de Metz', in *La Lorraine: études archéologiques (Actes du 103e congrès national des Sociétés savantes (Nancy–Metz, 1978), Section d'archaeologie et d'histoire de l'art)*, Paris, 1980, pp. 27–62, esp. pp. 50–59.

35. David King, 'Medieval Art in Norfolk and the Continent: An Overview', in David Bates and Robert Liddiard, eds, *East Anglia and its North Sea World in the Middle Ages*, Woodbridge, 2013, pp. 82–119.

36. For example at f. 274r of the winter portion of Renaud's Breviary, see www.bl.uk/catalogues/illuminatedmanuscripts/record.asp?MSID=811 4&CollID=58&NStart=8 (accessed 3 September 2014).

37. I will return to this subject in my forthcoming article on the artists of the Ormesby Psalter.

38. Oxford, Bodleian Library MS. Ashmole 1523; Cambridge, Emmanuel College MS 112; Dublin, Trinity College MS 64. See Sandler, *Gothic Manuscripts*, vol. 2, pp. 51–3, nos. 44–46. For the Emmanuel Moralia, see also Paul Binski and Stella Panayotova, eds, *The Cambridge Illuminations: Ten Centuries of Book Production in the Medieval West*, London and Turnhout, 2005, pp. 104–5, no. 35.

39. Norwich, Castle Museum MS 158.926.4f, which contains an almanac calculation for 1339 on fol. 8v; Cambridge, Fitzwilliam Museum MS. 379; London, British Library Royal MS 14.C.1. See Sandler, *Gothic Manuscripts*, vol. 2, pp. 53–6, nos 47–49.

40. Ian Tyers, 'Tree-ring Analysis', *Painting and Practice: The Thornham Parva Retable. Technique, Conservation and Context of an English Medieval Painting*, London and Turnhout, 200, pp. 113–21. An alternative provenance with the Dominicans of Norwich has recently been proposed by Nicholas Rogers, 'The Provenance of the Thornham Parva Retable', *The Friars in Medieval Britain: Proceedings of the 2007 Harlaxton Symposium*, Harlaxton Medieval Studies, vol. XIX, ed. Nicholas Rogers, Donington, 2010, pp. 185–94. My thanks to Nicholas Rogers for sending me a copy of this article.

41. Martial Rose and Julia Hedgecoe, *Stories in Stone: The Medieval Roof Carvings of Norwich Cathedral*, London, 1997, p. 30.

42. It is fascinating that the styles of both of the principal artists of the Ormesby Psalter can be paralleled in the first phase of the sculpture of the Cathedral Cloister, raising questions as to the range of skills of the craftsman involved, and to whether a seemingly individual style can be associated with a particular artist or group of artists, or simply represents a local style practised by a number of artists working in different media.

43. London, Lambeth Palace Library MS 233. See Sandler, *Gothic Manuscripts*, vol. 2, pp. 35–6, no. 30.

44. Donald Drew Egbert, *The Tickhill Psalter and Related Manuscripts*, New York, 1940, p. 115.

45. London, British Library Arundel MS 83 1. See Sandler, *Gothic Manuscripts*, vol. 2, pp. 58–60, no. 51.

46. Nicholas Harris Nicolas, *The Siege of Carlaverock in the XVIII Edward I. A.D. MCCC; with the Arms of the Earls, Barons and Knights who were present on the occasion; with a translation, a history of the castle, and memoirs of the personages commemorated by the poet,* London, 1828, p. 7.

47. Biblioteca del Escorial MS Q II 6. See Sandler, *Gothic Manuscripts*, vol. 2, pp. 87–9, no. 80.

48. Fairbank F. Royston, 'The Last Earl of Warenne and Surrey and the Distribution of His Possessions', *Yorkshire Archaeological Journal* 19, 1906–7, pp. 193–264. On the Seagraves/Segraves, see S. Hamilton, 'Seagrave , Nicholas (d. 1321)', *Oxford Dictionary of National Biography*, Oxford, 2004, online at www.oxforddnb.com/view/article/25040 (accessed 2 September 2014); A.J. Musson, 'Seagrave, John, second Lord Seagrave (1256–1325)', *Oxford Dictionary of National Biography*, Oxford, 2004, online at www.oxforddnb.com.library/view/article/25038 (accessed 11 September 2014).

49. The window, which was described by Blomefield, is no longer extant although glass with the Foliot arms survives. See 'Eynford Hundred: Elsing', *An Essay towards a Topographical History of the County of Norfolk*, vol. 8, pp. 201–3; www.british-history.ac.uk/report.aspx?compid=78448&strquery=Elsing Norfolk (accessed 2 September 2014).

50. See Linda Dennison and Nicholas Rogers, 'The Elsing Brass and Its East Anglian Connections', in *Fourteenth Century England*, vol. I, ed. Nigel Saul, Woodbridge, 2000, pp. 167–93.

51. Cambridge, Corpus Christi College MS 465. See J.B.L. Tolhurst, *The Customary of the Cathedral Priory Church at Norwich, MS 465 in the Library of Corpus Christi College, Cambridge*, London, 1948.

52. Richard Sharpe, 'Accession, Classification, Location: Shelfmarks in Medieval Libraries', *Scriptorium*, L, 1996, pp. 279–87, esp. p. 284.

53. On books with the A pressmark, see N.R. Ker, 'Medieval Manuscripts from Norwich Cathedral Priory', in his *Books, Collectors and Libraries: Studies in Medieval Heritage*, ed. Andrew G. Watson, London, 1985, pp. 243–71, esp. 247–53.

54. Richard Gameson, 'The Medieval Library (to *c.* 1450)', in *The Cambridge History of the Libraries in Britain and Ireland*, vol. 1: *To 1640*, ed. Elisabeth Leedham-Green and Teresa Webber, Cambridge, 2006, pp. 13–50, p. 38.

55. Joan Greatrex, 'Monk Students from Norwich Cathedral Priory *c.* 1300 to 1530', *English Historical Review* 106, 1991, pp. 555–83.

56. A.B. Emden, *A Biographical Register of the University of Cambridge to 1500*, Cambridge, 1963, p. 435, implies that Robert was a student at Cambridge, but Norwich rarely sent students there before the fifteenth century, and his appearance before a magistrate must have been long after his student days.

57. John Salmon's visitation of the Priory in 1308 had commented adversely on the punctuality of the monks and suggested the installation of a clock. See E.H. Carter, *Studies in Norwich Cathedral History: An Episcopal Visitation of the Priory in 1308 and an Archiepiscopal Adjudication on Priory Rights in 1411*, Norwich, 1935, p. 10.

58. Cambridge, University Library MS Kk.4.3. See Binski and Zutshi with Panayotova, *Western Illuminated Manuscripts*, pp. 108–9, no. 115.

59. E. Rutledge, 'Economic Life', in C. Rawcliffe and R. Wilson, eds, *Medieval Norwich*, London, 2004, pp. 156–88.

60. Cf. Lynda Dennison, 'Flemish Influence on English Manuscript Painting in East Anglia in the Fourteenth Century', in David Bates and Robert Liddiard, eds, *East Anglia and Its North Sea World in the Middle Ages*, Woodbridge, 2013, p. 334.

SUGGESTED READING

A list of all published references to the Ormesby Psalter is outside the scope and intentions of this work, but it is hoped that some indication of further directions for interested readers might be of use. This study is largely based on my Ph.D. dissertation, *Artists, Patrons and the Sequence of Production in the Ormesby Psalter (Oxford, Bodleian Library MS. Douce 366)* (Courtauld Institute of Art, University of London, 1999), where a fuller bibliography can be found. Although the ideas expressed there are basically those of the present work, new material has come to light since then and there have been some revised attributions.

The most important studies of the manuscript remain S.C. Cockerell and M.R. James, *Two East Anglian Psalters at the Bodleian Library, Oxford* (Oxford, 1926), and more recently the catalogue entry in Lucy Freeman Sandler, *Gothic Manuscripts 1285–1385*, 2 vols (volume V in *A Survey of Manuscripts Illuminated in the British Isles*, gen. ed. J.J.G Alexander, London, 1986), vol. 2, pp. 49–51, no. 43; vol. 1, colour frontispiece and illus. 96–8. Significant contributions to identifying the different campaigns were also made in E.W.B. Nicholson's revisions to Falconer Madan, *Summary Catalogue of Western Manuscripts in the Bodleian Library at Oxford*, vol. V (Oxford, 1905), pp. xxii–xxviii, no. 21941; Donald Drew Egbert, *The Tickhill Psalter and Related Manuscripts: A School of Manuscript Illumination in England during the Early Fourteenth Century* (New York, 1940), pp. 112–16, 209–18 Appendix VII, pl. CX; O. Pächt, 'A Giottesque Episode in English Medieval Art', *Journal of the Warburg and Courtauld Institutes* 6, 1943, pp. 51–70; P. Lasko and N.J. Morgan, eds, *Medieval Art in East Anglia 1300–1520* (exhibition catalogue, Norwich, 1973), pp. 18–19, no. 21; Lucy Freeman Sandler's catalogue entry for the manuscript in *Age of Chivalry: Art in Plantagenet England 1200–1400*, ed. Jonathan Alexander and Paul Binski (exhibition catalogue, Royal Academy of Arts, London, 1987), p. 454, no. 573.

Studies of specific aspects of the iconography include Lucy Freeman Sandler, 'A Bawdy Betrothal in the Ormesby Psalter', *Tribute to Lotte Brand Philip* (New York, 1985), pp. 155–9, and F. Law-Turner, 'Beasts, Benedictines and the Ormesby Master: Pictorial Exegesis in English Fourteenth-century Manuscript Illumination', *British Art Journal* 1, Autumn 1999, pp. 5–13. For a recent discussion of Jesse Trees with Coronations and Annunciations, see Elizabeth Valdez del Álamo, *Palace of the Mind: The Cloister of Silos and Spanish Sculpture of the Twelfth Century* (Turnhout, 2012), pp. 260–89. On Psalter illustration in England in the period under discussion, see C.M. Kauffmann, *Biblical Imagery in Medieval England 700–1550* (London and Turnhout, 2003), pp. 147–90, 207–42; Lucy Freeman Sandler, *The Peterborough Psalter in Brussels and Other Fenland Manuscripts* (London, 1974), and her 'Images of Words in English Gothic Psalters (The Saunders Lecture, 1997)', in Brendan Cassidy and Rosemary Muir Wright, eds, *Studies in the Illustration of the Psalter* (Stamford CT, 2000), pp. 67–86. On French illuminated psalters, see E.A. Peterson, *Iconography of the Historiated Psalm Initials in the 13th Century French Fully-Illustrated Psalter Group* (Ph.D. dissertation, University of Pittsburgh, 1991), and her 'The Textual Basis for Visual Errors in French Gothic Psalter Illustration', in Richard Gameson, ed., *The Early Medieval Bible: Its Production, Decoration and Use* (Cambridge, 1994), pp. 177–204; and her 'Scholastic Hermeneutics in Historiated Initials of 13th-Century French Psalters', in F.O. Büttner, ed., *The Illuminated Psalter: Studies in Context, Purpose and Placement of its Images* (Turnhout, 2005), pp. 349–60. The patronage and use of English psalters in the thirteenth century is studied by Nigel Morgan, 'Patrons and their Devotions in the Historiated Initials and Full-Page Miniatures of 13th-Century English Psalters', in Büttner, ed., *The Illuminated Psalter*, pp. 309–22.

On medieval bindings, see Michael Gullick and Nicholas Hadgraft, 'Bookbindings', in 'The Technology of Production of the Manuscript Book', in *The Cambridge History of the Book in Britain*, Volume III: *1100–1400*, ed. Nigel Morgan and Rodney M. Thomson (Cambridge, 2008), pp. 95–109. On painted fore-edges, see Miriam Foot, 'Medieval Painted Book Edges', in J.L. Sharpe, ed., *Roger Powell, the Compleat Binder: Liber amicorum* (Turnhout, 1996), pp. 260–67.

On the East Anglian school, see Lasko and Morgan, eds, *Medieval Art in East Anglia 1300–1520*, pp. 7, 18–25, nos 20–28; Lucy Freeman Sandler, *Gothic Manuscripts*, vol. 1, pp. 27–30, and relevant entries in vol. 2 with bibliographies; Nigel J. Morgan and Lucy Freeman Sandler, 'Manuscript Illumination of the Thirteenth and Fourteenth Centuries', in *Age of Chivalry*, ed. Alexander and Binski, pp. 153–4; Caroline Susan Hull, *The Douai Psalter and Related Manuscripts* (Ph.D. dissertation, Yale University, 1994) and her article 'Abbot John, Vicar Thomas and M.R. James: The Early History of the Douai Psalter', in Lynda Dennison, ed., *The Legacy of M.R. James: Papers from the 1995 Cambridge Symposium* (Donington, 2001), pp. 118–27; M.A. Michael, 'Oxford, Cambridge and London: Towards a Theory for Grouping Gothic manuscripts', *Burlington Magazine* 130, 1988, pp. 107–15; 'Deconstruction, Reconstruction and Invention: The Hungerford Hours and English Manuscript Illumination of the Early Fourteenth Century', in P. Beal and J. Griffiths, eds, *English Studies 1100–1700*, vol. 2, 1990, pp. 33–108;

'Seeing-in: The Macclesfield Psalter', in S. Panayotova, ed., *The Cambridge Illuminations: The Conference Papers* (London and Turnhout, 2007), pp. 115–28; Lilian M.C. Randall, 'Sense and Sensibilities in an Early Fourteenth-century Psalter from East Anglia', in Panayotova, ed., *The Cambridge Illuminations*, pp. 219–233; Stella Panayotova, *The Macclesfield Psalter* (Cambridge, 2008), pp. 20–27. The development of manuscript painting in the second half of the fourteenth century has recently been dealt with by Lucy Freeman Sandler, *Illuminators and Patrons in Fourteenth-Century England: The Psalter and Hours of Humphrey de Bohun and the Manuscripts of the Bohun Family* (London and Toronto, 2014), and by Lynda Dennison, 'Flemish Influence on English Manuscript Painting in East Anglia in the Fourteenth Century', in David Bates and Robert Liddiard, eds, *East Anglia and Its North Sea World in the Middle Ages* (Woodbridge, 2013), pp. 315–35.

On Messin manuscripts, see Alison Stones, *Gothic Manuscripts 1260–1320*, in *A Survey of Manuscripts Illuminated in France*, Part 1, vol. 1 (London and Turnhout, 2013), pp. 39–41, 71–2; Part 2, vol. 1 (London and Turnhout, 2014), pp. 21–88, IV: Province of Trier and Duchy of Lorraine, County of Bar, Metz and Verdun; and her 'Les manuscrits de Renaud de Bar', in Ann-Orange Poilpré and Marianne Besseyre, eds, *L'écrit et le livre peint en Lorraine, de Saint-Mihiel à Verdun (IXe–XVe siècles): Actes du colloque de Saint-Mihiel (25–26 octobre 2010)* (Turnhout, 2014), pp. 269–310; François Avril in *L'art au temps des Rois Maudits, Philippe le Bel et ses fils 1285–1328* (exhibition catalogue, Paris, 1998), pp. 314–18, nos 214–16. The link between the Ormesby Psalter and the de Bar manuscripts was first observed by Patrick M. de Winter, 'Une réalisation exceptionnelle d'enlumineurs français et anglais vers 1300: Le Bréviaire de Renaud de Bar, Évêque de Metz', in *La Lorraine, Études archéologiques, Archéologie et histoire de l'art* (Paris, 1980), pp. 28–62. The main study of the de Bar manuscripts remains Sharon Kay Davenport, *Manuscripts Illuminated for Renaud of Bar, Bishop of Metz (1303–1316)* (Ph.D. dissertation, Courtauld Institute of Art, University of London, 1984).

On the sculpted decoration of Norwich Cathedral Cloister, the Prior's Door and the Ethelbert Gate, see Eric Fernie, *An Architectural History of Norwich Cathedral* (Oxford, 1993), pp. 163–81; Francis Woodman, 'The Gothic Campaigns', in Ian Atherton, Eric Fernie et al., eds, *Norwich Cathedral: Church, City and Diocese* (London and Rio Grande OH, 1996), pp. 165–78; Veronica Sekules, 'The Gothic Sculpture', in Atherton, Fernie et al., eds, *Norwich Cathedral*, pp. 199–202; Veronica Sekules, 'Religious Politics and the Cloister Bosses of Norwich Cathedral', in Martin Henig and John McNeil, eds, *The Medieval Cloister in England and Wales* (Leeds, 2006), pp. 284–306; Roberta Gilchrist, *Norwich Cathedral Close: The Evolution of the English Cathedral Landscape* (Woodbridge, 2005), pp. 77–92. On the church of St Margaret at Cley-next-the-Sea, see Richard

SUGGESTED READING **153**

Fawcett, 'The Influence of the Gothic Parts of the Cathedral on Church Building in Norfolk', in Atherton, Fernie et al., eds, *Norwich Cathedral*, pp. 210–29. On the thirteenth-century wall paintings in Norwich Cathedral, see Paul Binski, 'The Ante-Reliquary Chapel Paintings in Norwich Cathedral: The Holy Blood, St Richard and All Saints', in Julian M. Luxford and M.A. Michael, eds, *Tributes to Nigel Morgan. Contexts of Medieval Art: Images, Objects & Ideas* (Turnhout, 2010), pp. 241–63. On Norwich and Norfolk stained glass, see David King, *Stained Glass Tours around Norfolk Churches* (1974); and his 'Stained Glass', in Carol Rawcliffe and Richard Wilson, eds, *Medieval Norwich* (Hambledon and London, 2004), pp. 121–36; and his 'Late Medieval Glass Painting in Norfolk – Developments in Iconography and Craft', in T.A. Heslop, Elizabeth Mellings and Magrit Thofner, eds, *Art, Faith and Place in East Anglia from Pre-History to the Present* (Woodbridge, 2012), pp. 130–47. On the Thornham Parva Retable, see A. Massing, ed., *The Thornham Parva Retable: Technique, Conservation and Context of an English Medieval Painting* (Cambridge, 2003). The standard work on the Retable remains C. Norton, D. Park and P. Binski, *Dominican Painting in East Anglia: The Thornham Parva Retable and the Musée de Cluny Frontal* (Woodbridge, 1987).

For the history of Norwich Cathedral Priory and its library, see Neil Ker, 'Medieval Manuscripts from Norwich Cathedral Priory', repr. in his *Books, Collectors and Libraries: Studies in the Medieval Heritage*, ed. Andrew G. Watson (London and Ronceverte, 1985), pp. 243–71; *English Benedictine Libraries, The Shorter Catalogues, Corpus of British Medieval Library Catalogues*, vol. 4, ed. R. Sharpe, J.P. Carley, R.M. Thomson and A.G. Watson (London, 1996), pp. 288–91; various essays in Atherton, Fernie et al., *Norwich Cathedral*, in particular Barbara Dodwell, 'The Monastic Community', pp. 231–54 and 'The Muniments and Library', pp. 325–38, and Ralph Holbrooke, 'Refoundation and Reformation, 1538–1628', pp. 507–39. N. Ker, ed., *Medieval Libraries of Great Britain: A List of Surviving Books* (2nd edn, London, 1964), pp. 135–9, and *Supplement to the Second Edition*, ed. Andrew G. Watson (London, 1987), pp. 50–51, list surviving manuscripts from Norwich with current locations, including the Ormesby Psalter. On the Norwich system of pressmarks, see Richard Sharpe, 'Accession, Classification, Location: Shelfmarks in Medieval Libraries', *Scriptorium*, L, 1996, pp. 270–87, esp. p. 284. For the modern history of the Ormesby Psalter, see S.G. Gillam, ed., *The Douce Legacy: An Exhibition to Commemorate the 150th Anniversary of the Bequest of Francis Douce (1757–1834)* (Oxford, 1984), pp. 167–8, no. 244.

The histories of the Bardolf, Foliot and Ormesby families have been reconstructed from published sources, both primary and secondary. The Earls of Warenne and some members of the Bardolf and Foliot families merit entries in the *Oxford Dictionary of National Biography*, at www.oxforddnb.com. All appear in G.E. Cockayne,

The Complete Peerage of England, Scotland, Ireland, Great Britain and the United Kingdom, Extant, Extinct or Dormant (new edn by V. Gibbs, ed., 13 vols, London, 1910–88). The Foliot family has recently been studied by D. Crook, 'Jordan Castle and the Foliot family of Grimston, 1225–1330', *Transactions of the Thoroton Society* CXII, 2008, pp. 143–58. Also of great use are F. Blomefield, *An Essay towards a Topographical History of the County of Norfolk* (2nd edn, 11 vols, 1805–10); G.A. Carthew, *The Hundred of Launditch and the Deanery of Brisley in the County of Norfolk* (3 vols, 1877–79); Arthur H. Doubleday and William Page, *Victoria County History for Norfolk*, vol. 2 (London, 1906); C. Moor, *Knights of Edward* I (5 vols, 1929–32); I.J. Sanders, *English Baronies: A Study of their Origin and Descent 1086–1327* (Oxford, 1960); Charles Clay, 'Hugh Bardolf the Justice and his Family', *Lincolnshire History and Archaeology* 1, 1966, pp. 5–28; E. Hallam, *The Itinerary of Edward II and His Household, 1307–1328*, List and Index Society Publications 211 (Kew, 1984).

Much information about the two families was derived from the published medieval records, including the various records held by the Norfolk Record Office, searchable at www.archives.norfolk.gov.uk; the *Calendars of Inquisitions Post Mortem*, gen. ed. Christine Carpenter (Woodbridge, 2003–11), pp. xxii–xxvi; *Parliamentary writs and writs of military summons: together with the records and muniments relating to the suit and service due and performed to the King's high court of Parliament and the councils of the realm, or affording evidence of attendance given at Parliament and councils* (2 vols, ed. F. Palgrave, 1827–34); *Inquisitions and Assessments relating to Feudal Aids, with other analogous documents, preserved in the Public Record Office A.D. 1284–1431* (6 vols, 1899–1920); *Calendar of the Patent Rolls Preserved in the Public Record Office, Edward I, Edward II and Edward III* (16 vols, 1893–1916); *Calendar of the Charter Rolls Preserved in the Public Record Office, Henry III–Henry VIII, 1226–1516* (6 vols, 1903–27); *Calendar of the Close Rolls Preserved in the Public Record Office, Edward I, Edward II & Edward III* (21 vols, 1904–13); *Calendar of the Inquisitions Post Mortem and other Analogous Deeds Preserved in the Public Record Office, Henry III, Edward I, Edward II & Edward III* (14 vols, 1904–52); *Calendar of the Fine Rolls Preserved in the Public Record Office, Edward I, Edward II & Edward III, 1327–1347* (6 vols, 1911–21); *Calendar of Inquisitions Miscellaneous (Chancery) Preserved in the Public Record Office*, vol. 11, 1916; *Year Books of Edward II*, vol. xxv, 12 Edward II, part of *Easter and Trinity 1319* (ed. John P. Collins, 1964); *Records of the Wardrobe and Household 1286–9* (2 vols, ed. B. Byerly and C. Ridder Byerly, 1977–87).

On John de Warenne and his family connections, see initially Scott L. Waugh, 'Warenne, John de, Seventh Earl of Surrey (1286–1347)', *Oxford Dictionary of National Biography* (2004; online edn, May 2008, www.oxforddnb.com/index/101028735/John-de-Warenne, accessed 2 September 2014), and other relevant entries, and the relevant entry in the *Complete Peerage*. His patronage has been studied by Margot M. Nishimura and David Nishimura, 'Rabbits, Warrens and Warenne: The Patronage of the Gorleston Psalter', in Kathryn A. Smith and Carol H. Krinsky, eds, *Tributes to Lucy Freeman Sandler: Studies in Illuminated Manuscripts* (London and Turnhout, 2007), pp. 205–17; David King, 'John de Warenne, Edmund de Gonville and the Thetford Dominican Altar Paintings', in Julian M. Luxford and M.A. Michael, eds, *Tributes to Nigel Morgan. Contexts in Medieval Art: Images, Objects and Ideas* (London and Turnhout, 2010), pp. 293–306. The extent and nature of Warenne's artistic interests justify further study; I hope to return to this at a later date.

On Robert of Ormesby, see A.B. Emden, *A Biographical Register of the University of Cambridge to 1500* (Cambridge, 1963), p. 435; D. Knowles, *The Monastic Order in England: A History of Its Development from the Times of St. Dunstan to the 4th Lateran Council 940–1216* (2nd edn, Cambridge, 1966); Joan Greatrex, 'Monk Students from Norwich Cathedral Priory at Oxford and Cambridge, *c.* 1300 to 1530', *English Historical Review* 106, 1991, pp. 555–83, and *Biographical Register of the English Cathedral Priories of the Province of Canterbury c. 1066–1540* (Oxford, 1997), p. 546; David M. Smith and Vera C.M. London, eds, *The Heads of Religious Houses in England and Wales II 1216–1377* (Cambridge, 2001), p. 112.

For the general history of the period, see M. Prestwich, *The Three Edwards: War and State in England 1272–1377* (2nd edn, Abingdon, 2003), and the same author's *Edward I* (2nd edn, New Haven CT and London, 1997); J.R. Maddicott, *Thomas of Lancaster 1307–1322: A Study in the Reign of Edward II* (Oxford, 1970); Seymour Phillips, *Edward II* (New Haven CT and London, 2010); Ian Mortimer, *The Perfect King: The Life of Edward III, Father of the Nation* (London, 2006). An extremely engaging account of Edward II's reign can be found in Ian Mortimer, *The Greatest Traitor: The Life of Sir Roger Mortimer, First Earl of March, Ruler of England 1327–1330* (London, 2003).

LIST OF ILLUSTRATIONS

FIGURE 1 Ormesby Psalter (Oxford, Bodleian Library MS. Douce 366), fol. 1v, inscription recording the donation of the manuscript to Norwich Cathedral Priory by Robert of Ormesby

FIGURE 2 Ormesby Psalter (Oxford, Bodleian Library MS. Douce 366), chemise binding, closed

FIGURE 3 Gorleston Psalter (London, British Library Additional MS. 49622), fol. 8r, Psalm 1, *Beatus* initial with Jesse Tree, *c.* 1310–20

FIGURE 4 Ormesby Psalter (Oxford, Bodleian Library MS. Douce 366), fol. 16v, Gothic liturgical hand and penwork line fillers, late-thirteenth-century campaign

FIGURE 5 Ormesby Psalter (Oxford, Bodleian Library MS. Douce 366), fol. 10v, Psalm 2, Q initial with David debating with a group of men, late-thirteenth-century campaign

FIGURE 6 Ormesby Psalter (Oxford, Bodleian Library MS. Douce 366), fol. 12r, Psalm 4, C initial with David kneeling before an altar, late-thirteenth-century campaign

FIGURE 7 Ormesby Psalter (Oxford, Bodleian Library MS. Douce 366), fol. 16r, Psalm 8, S initial, late-thirteenth-century campaign

FIGURE 8 Ormesby Psalter (Oxford, Bodleian Library MS. Douce 366), fol. 20r, Psalm 10, I initial with the Ascension, late-thirteenth-century campaign

FIGURE 9 Bible of Richard of Felmingham (Oxford, Bodleian Library MS. Auct. D.4.8), fol. 366v, D initial, Solomon enthroned above conquered kings, East Anglia, mid-thirteenth century

FIGURE 10 Blackburn Psalter, Blackburn Museum and Art Gallery MS. Hart 21001, fol. 13r, *Beatus* page, Oxford(?), *c.* 1260–80

FIGURE 11 Ormesby Psalter (Oxford, Bodleian Library MS. Douce 366), fol. 13r, Psalm 5, V initial with David pointing to his mouth, late-thirteenth-century campaign

FIGURE 12 Ormesby Psalter (Oxford, Bodleian Library MS. Douce 366), fol. 16r, Psalm 8, D initial with a man holding a globe of the world, late-thirteenth-century campaign

FIGURE 13 Ormesby Psalter (Oxford, Bodleian Library MS. Douce 366), fol. 11v, Psalm 3, D initial with the Resurrection, late-thirteenth-century campaign

FIGURE 14 Ormesby Psalter (Oxford, Bodleian Library MS. Douce 366), fol. 9v, detail of Foliot and Bardolf donor figures, 1310s campaign

FIGURE 15 Ormesby Psalter (Oxford, Bodleian Library MS. Douce 366), fol. 38r, Psalm 26, D initial with knight in upright bearing variant on Foliot arms, and adjoining lines with Warenne arms in line filler, 1310s campaign

FIGURE 16 Ormesby Psalter (Oxford, Bodleian Library MS. Douce 366), fol. 128r, Psalm 97, lower border with Foliot knight fighting a dragon, 1310s campaign

FIGURE 17 Ormesby Psalter (Oxford, Bodleian Library MS. Douce 366), fol. 154r, Foliot and Bardolf arms in line fillers, 1310s campaign

FIGURE 18 Ormesby Psalter (Oxford, Bodleian Library MS. Douce 366), fols 9v and 10r, the double *Beatus* opening, 1310s and 1330s campaigns

FIGURE 19 Norwich Cathedral Cloister, Prior's Door, *c.* 1300–20, Christ flanked by angels and saints

FIGURE 20 St Peter's, Lowick, Northamptonshire, stained-glass figures of prophets from a Jesse window, *c.* 1317

FIGURE 21 Macclesfield Psalter (Cambridge, Fitzwilliam Museum MS. 1–2005), fol. 9r, Psalm 1 *Beatus* page with Tree of Jesse, *c.* 1325–30

FIGURE 22 Ormesby Psalter (Oxford, Bodleian Library MS. Douce 366), fol. 24r, Collect for Psalm 15, C initial with bellows player in margin, 1310s campaign

FIGURE 23 Ormesby Psalter (Oxford, Bodleian Library MS. Douce 366), fol. 23v, Psalm 15, C initial with Last Judgement, 1310s campaign

FIGURE 24 Ormesby Psalter (Oxford, Bodleian Library MS. Douce 366), fol. 37r, Psalm 25, L initial with bearded male head, 1310s campaign

FIGURE 25 Ormesby Psalter (Oxford, Bodleian Library MS. Douce 366), fol. 41r, Psalm 29, E initial with Jew asperging a temple, 1310s campaign

FIGURE 26 Ormesby Psalter (Oxford, Bodleian Library MS. Douce 366), fol. 35v, Psalm 24, A initial with kneeling bearded man, 1310s campaign

FIGURE 27 Ormesby Psalter (Oxford, Bodleian Library MS. Douce 366), fol. 29r, Psalm 18, C initial with Virgin and Child, 1310s campaign

FIGURE 28 Ormesby Psalter (Oxford, Bodleian Library MS. Douce 366), fol. 30r, Psalm 19, E initial with Sacrifice of Isaac, 1310s campaign

FIGURE 29 Ormesby Psalter (Oxford, Bodleian Library MS. Douce 366), fol. 32r, Psalm 21, D initial, Crucifixion, 1310s campaign

FIGURE 30 Ormesby Psalter (Oxford, Bodleian Library MS. Douce 366), fol. 44r, Psalm 31, B initial, youth confessing to a friar, 1310s campaign

FIGURE 31 Ormesby Psalter (Oxford, Bodleian Library MS. Douce 366), fol. 50r, Ormesby Master underdrawings from 1310s campaign overpainted by Cheap Finisher

FIGURE 32 Ormesby Psalter (Oxford, Bodleian Library MS. Douce 366, fol. 147v, detail of naked trumpeter and battle between lion and bear

FIGURE 33 Breviary of Renaud de Bar (Verdun, Bibliothèque municipale MS. 107), fol. 12r, *bas-de-page* figures of a young woman playing a rebec, and man and woman with falcon, before 1316

FIGURE 34 Bromholm Psalter (Oxford, Bodleian Library Ashmole MS 1523), fol. 66r, Psalm 52, D initial with a fool and a man debating, *c.* 1310–20

FIGURE 35 Macclesfield Psalter (Cambridge, Fitzwilliam Museum MS 1–2005), fol. 39r, *c.* 1325–30

FIGURE 36 Thornham Parva Retable (St Mary's, Thornham Parva, Suffolk), after 1317

FIGURE 37 Norwich Cathedral Cloister, roof boss, *c.* 1310–20

FIGURE 38 Cley-next-the-Sea, St Margaret's, Norfolk, musician, *c.* 1310–20

FIGURE 39 Norwich Cathedral, Ethelbert Gate, after 1316

FIGURE 40 St Peter's, Ringland, Norfolk, musical centaur, *c.* 1310–20

FIGURE 41 Ormesby Psalter (Oxford, Bodleian Library MS. Douce 366), fol. 48r, Psalm 34, Ormesby Master underdrawings from 1310s campaign overpainted by Cheap Finisher

FIGURE 42 Ormesby Psalter (Oxford, Bodleian Library MS. Douce 366), fols 64v and 65r, Psalms 45 and 46, D and P initials and borders, 1310s campaign

FIGURE 43 Breviary of Renaud de Bar (Verdun, Bibliothèque municipale MS. 107), fol. 285v, before 1316

FIGURE 44 Ormesby Psalter (Oxford, Bodleian Library MS. Douce 366), fol. 66r, Psalm 47, M initial with Christ and the Heavenly Jerusalem, 1310s campaign

FIGURE 45 Ormesby Psalter (Oxford, Bodleian Library MS. Douce 366), fol. 58r, collect to Psalm 39, E initial with hare and magpie in border, 1310s campaign

FIGURE 46 Ormesby Psalter (Oxford, Bodleian Library MS. Douce 366), fols 80v and 81r, D initial, 1310s campaign

FIGURE 47 Stowe Breviary, D initial, St Michael and the dragon (London, British Library Stowe MS. 12), fol. 305r, 1322–25

FIGURE 48 St Omer Psalter (London, British Library Yates Thompson MS. 14), fol. 8r, D initial with decorative border, *c.* 1330–40

FIGURE 49 Ormesby Psalter (Oxford, Bodleian Library Douce MS. Douce 366), fol. 190r, Canticle of Isaiah, underdrawings from 1310s campaign overpainted by Cheap Finisher

FIGURE 50 Ormesby Psalter (Oxford, Bodleian Library Douce MS. Douce 366), fols 155v and 156r, Psalm 118, underdrawing and partial illumination from 1310s campaign, overpainted by Cheap Finisher

FIGURE 51 Vaux-Bardolf Psalter with bar border and grotesque terminal (London, Lambeth Palace Library MS. 233), fol. 23v, *c.* 1310–20

FIGURE 52 Ormesby Psalter (Oxford, Bodleian Library MS. Douce 366), fols 194v and 195r, Canticle of Habbakuk, 1310s campaign

FIGURE 53 Castle Acre, Norfolk, remains of the castle

FIGURE 54 Ormesby Psalter (Oxford, Bodleian Library MS. Douce 366), fol. 6r, September, with the feast of the Dedication of Norwich Cathedral in gold, 1330s campaign

FIGURE 55 Ormesby Psalter (Oxford, Bodleian Library MS. Douce 366), fol. 8v, the erased donation inscription

FIGURE 56 Ormesby Psalter (Oxford, Bodleian Library MS. Douce 366), fol. 210r, the second Litany, with double invocations of William of Norwich and St Benedict, 1330s campaign

FIGURE 57 St Omer Psalter (London, British Library Yates Thompson MS. 14), fol. 57v, Psalm 52, initial D with David enthroned debating with a fool, *c.* 1330–40; initial B, Ormesby Psalter (Oxford, Bodleian Library MS. Douce 366), fol. 10r

FIGURE 58 Ormesby Psalter (Oxford, Bodleian Library MS. Douce 366), inside of back cover

FIGURE 59 Ormesby Psalter (Oxford, Bodleian Library MS. Douce 366), fol. 2r, detail of shelfmarks

FIGURE 60 Ormesby Psalter (Oxford, Bodleian Library MS. Douce 366), painted fore-edges, after 1340

FIGURE 61 Ormesby Psalter (Oxford, Bodleian Library MS. Douce 366), chemise binding shown open at fols 64v–65r

PLATE 1 Ormesby Psalter (Oxford, Bodleian Library MS. Douce 366), fol. 9v

PLATE 2 Ormesby Psalter (Oxford, Bodleian Library MS. Douce 366), fol. 10r

PLATE 3 Ormesby Psalter (Oxford, Bodleian Library MS. Douce 366), fol. 38r

PLATE 4 Ormesby Psalter (Oxford, Bodleian Library MS. Douce 366), fol. 55v

PLATE 5 Ormesby Psalter (Oxford, Bodleian Library MS. Douce 366), fol. 71v

PLATE 6 Ormesby Psalter (Oxford, Bodleian Library MS. Douce 366), fol. 72r

PLATE 7 Ormesby Psalter (Oxford, Bodleian Library MS. Douce 366), fol. 89r

PLATE 8 Ormesby Psalter (Oxford, Bodleian Library MS. Douce 366), fol. 109r

PLATE 9 Ormesby Psalter (Oxford, Bodleian Library MS. Douce 366), fol. 128r

PLATE 10 Ormesby Psalter (Oxford, Bodleian Library MS. Douce 366), fol. 131r

PLATE 11 Ormesby Psalter (Oxford, Bodleian Library MS. Douce 366), fol. 147v

INDEX

References to illustrations are in bold

Aguillon family 74
Aguillon, Sir Robert 70
Aguillons Hall 74

Balliol, Edward 41
Balliol, John, king of Scotland 41
Balliol, Isabella *née* de Warenne 41
Balliol family 38
Bannockburn 29
Bar, Henri III, Comte de 48
Bar, Joan de, *see under* Joan de
    Warenne
Bar, Renaud de, Bishop of Metz
    46, 48, 59, 101, 115
    Breviary of, *see under* Breviary
Bardolf family of Wormegay 6, 25,
    27, 38, 41, 43, 61, 65, 66–76,
    79–82, 88, 100, 107
    Bardolf, Agnes, *née* de Grandson
        79
    Bardolf, Cecily, *see under* Morley
    Bardolf, Cecily, wife of Thomas
        79
    Bardolf, Hugh, 1st Baron 70,
        74, 75, 78
    Bardolf, Isabella, *née* Aguillon
        70, 74
    Bardolf, Joan 79
    Bardolf, John, 3rd Baron 80
    Bardolf, Robert 6, 74
    Bardolf, Thomas, 2nd Baron
        70, 77, 78, 79, 80, 81
    Bardolf, William, sheriff of
        Norfolk and Suffolk 70
    Bardolf, William 75
    see also Stoke Bardolph,
        Stow Bardolph
Becket, Thomas *see* Thomas, St
bestiaries 50. 113–15, 117, 136
Bible of Richard of Felmingham

18, 20
Blackburn Psalter 21
Bodleian Library 3, 4
Bohun family 38, 41, 79, 101
Bohun, James de 41, 79
Bohun, Joan de *see* Bardolf
Books of Hours 8, 50
Breviary of Renaud de Bar 48, 49,
    58, 59
Brewes, William de, Lord of
    Bamber and Gower 79
Bromholm Priory 48
Bromholm Psalter 50, 50
Burgh Vaux 74
Bury St Edmunds 80
Bussey family 80

Camoys, John de 82
Camoys, Margaret de, *née* Foliot
    79, 82
Carrow Psalter 18
Castile family 38, 41, 48
Castile, Eleanor of 41
Castle Acre, seat of Warenne
    family 76, 76, 77, 81
Cheap Finisher *see under* Ormesby
    Psalter
*Chronicles of the Roman Emperors and
    Popes* (Martinus Polonus) 50
Clare family 38, 41, 61, 65, 77
Clare, Gilbert de, Earl of
    Gloucester 41, 110
Clare, Margaret de, *see under*
    Gaveston
Cley-next-the-Sea, Church of
    St Margaret of Antioch 52, 53
Cockerell, Sir Sydney 4, 10, 98
Cornwall family 38, 41

Douai Psalter 9

Douce, Francis 3, 4
Douce Apocalypse 4
Duns Scotus (John Duns) 45
Dunstan, St 24
Edmund, St 24
Edward I, king of England 48, 70, 75, 78, 79, 88
Edward II, king of England 37, 41, 77, 79, 80, 88
Edward III, king of England 35, 100
Edward VI, king of England 3
Elsing, Church of St Mary 82
Ely Cathedral 124
Estuteville, Margery *see under* Foliot 75
Ethelbert, St 83
Etheldreda, St 83

Felix of Dunwich, St 83
Felmingham, Richard of 18, 20
Ferrers, William de, Earl of Derby 70
Fitzalan family 41, 61
Fitzalan, Alice, *née* de Warenne 41
Fitzalan, Edmund, Earl of Arundel 41
Fleggburgh 74
Foliot family of Gressenhall 6, 25, 27, 29, 35, 38, 41, 43, 61, 65, 66–76, 77, 79–82, 88, 100, 107, 110
Foliot, Beatrice, *née* Bardolf 74
Foliot, Joan, *née* de Brewes 79
Foliot, Jordan, 1st Lord 74, 75, 76, 128
Foliot, Margaret *see under* Camoys
Foliot, Margery, *née* Estuteville 75
Foliot, Margery, *née* Newmarch 41, 74, 75
Foliot, Margery, *see under* Hastings
Foliot, Richard (d. 1225) 74
Foliot, Richard, 2nd Lord 29, 41, 74, 75, 76, 77, 78, 79, 80, 81, 82, 100, 107, 110, 112, 128
Foliot, Richard, the younger 29, 41, 128
Foliot, William 75

Gaveston, Margaret, *née* de Clare 41

Gaveston, Piers, Count of Cornwall 41
Glossa ordinaria (Peter Lombard) 23, 24
Gloucester Cathedral 125
Gorleston, Franciscan Priory 45
Gorleston Psalter 4, 9, 10, 11, 61, 78, 81, 84, 101, 124, 125
Grandson, William de 79
Grantham Priory 45
Great Gloss (Peter Lombard) 23
Great Yarmouth 88
Gregory the Great, Pope 48
Moralia in Job 50
Gressenhall 75, 76, 81, 112
Guillaume le Clerc de Normandie 115

Hastings, Sir Hugh de 82
Hastings, Margery de, *née* Foliot 79, 82
Hastings, Isabel de 82
Hemenhale, Bishop Thomas 92, 107
Hereford Cathedral 125
Holme, St Benet's Abbey 51. 52, 91
Hours of Englebert of Nassau 4
Howard family, Earls of Suffolk 6
Howard Psalter 65
Hoxne Priory 92

Isabella, queen of England 80

Jesse Master *see under* Ormesby Psalter

Lancaster, Thomas, Earl of 29, 81, 82
Leon family 38
Lowick, Church St Peter 34, 34, 35
Ludlow, Church of St Laurence 125
Luttrell Psalter 125

Madrid, Biblioteca Nacional MS 6422 18
Macclesfield Psalter 9, 35, 35, 50, 51, 81
Margaret, queen of England 78
Metz 46, 48, 61, 101
Cathedral of St Étienne 46
paraiges (Jurue, Outre-Seille, Porte-Moselle) 61
see also Renauld de Bar

162   THE ORMESBY PSALTER

Morley, William, Lord 80
Morley, Cecily, *née* Bardolf 80
Mortimer, Roger 80

Neot, St 83
Nerford, Margaret de 41
Newmarch family 38, 41, 61
Newmarch, Margery de, *see under* Foliot
North Walsham 91
Norwich, Church of Holy Trinity 95
Norwich Book of Hours 50
Norwich Cathedral 3, 4, 6, 18, 33, 34, 50, 52, 53, 83, 87, 92, 100, 107
Norwich Cathedral Priory (Church of the Holy Trinity) 4, 9
    Ante-Reliquary Chapel, 18
    cloisters 34, 52
    Prior's Door 34, 19
    St Ethelbert Gate 52, 54

Ormesby, Agnes 91
Ormesby, John 91
Ormesby, Robert of 3, 4, 9, 83, 84, 88, 91, 92, 96, 98, 100, 107
Ormesby, Sir William de 74, 88
Ormesby, William, the younger 91
Ormesby 74, 88, 92
Ormesby Master *see under* Ormesby Psalter
Ormesby Psalter
    Beatus pages 4, 6, 25, 27, 29, 30–31, 32, 33, 105–9, 106, 109
    Calendar pages 3, 6, 16, 24, 83, 85, 87, 94, 95, 98
    Cheap Finisher 46, 54, 66, 70, 98
    chemise binding 4, 5, 6, 87, 97, 99
    coats of arms 6, 9, 25–9, 26, 28, 38–43, 39, 40, 42, 48, 60, 61–6, 62–3, 98–100, 99
    Crucifixion 44, 44, 84, 113, 115
    historiated initials 7, 21, 43, 61
    Jesse Master 29, 34, 32, 35, 38, 45
    Jesse Tree imagery 7, 30, 32–5, 82, 84, 105, 106
    King David imagery 15, 16, 17,
    22, 23, 24, 31, 32, 43, 61, 84, 91, 105, 107, 108, 109, 110, 111, 117, 119, 125, 131, 133, 136
    Last Judgement 23, 36, 37, 135
    Ormesby Master 45, 46, 48, 54, 59, 81, 113, 115, 117, 119, 122, 128
    St Omer Master 84
    Virgin and Child imagery 42, 43, 83
    zoomorphic imagery 7, 38, 61
Osyth, St 83

Pächt, Otto 46
Percy family 38, 41
Percy, Eleanor de, *née* de Warenne 41
Percy, Henry, 1st Baron 41
psalters *see under individual names*

Ringland, Church of St Peter 52, 54

St Benet's Abbey *see* Holme
St Étienne Cathedral *see* Metz
St Omer Master *see under* Ormesby Psalter
St Omer Psalter 9, 61, 65, 90, 91
St Omer, William de 84
Salmon, John, Bishop of Norwich 95
Saxlingham Nethergate 18
Scratby 74
Scratby Bardolphs 74
Segrave, Elizabeth 82
Segrave, John, Lord 82
Segrave, Nicholas 82
Segrave, Steven 82
Smithfield Decretals 136
Stoke Bardolph 70
Stow Bardolph 70, 74
Stowe Breviary 9, 61, 64, 65

Tewkesbury Abbey 37
Thetford Dominican Priory 50
Thomas Becket of Canterbury, St 3, 24, 83
Thornham Parva Retable 50, 52, 78, 81
Thorpe, Thomas 3
Tickhill, John, Prior of Worksop 25
Tickhill Psalter 24

INDEX 163

Ufford, Earls of Suffolk 9
  Ufford, Robert de 96, 100
Ufford family arms 9

Varenne family 41
Vaux family 41, 65, 70, 74, 80
Vaux, Petronilla de 41
Vaux, Roger de 75
Vaux-Bardolf Psalter 41, 65, 70, 71
Warenne family of Castle Acre 27,
  29, 38, 41, 43, 48, 61, 66, 70,
  75–82, 101, 107, 112
  see also Varenne

Warenne, John de, 6th Earl of
  Surrey and Sussex 25, 27, 29,
  38, 41, 45, 48, 50, 76, 77, 78,
  79, 81, 100, 101, 107, 112
Warenne, Joan de, *née* de Bar
  48
William of Norwich, St 83, 84, 88
Wormegay, seat of Bardolf family
  70, 74, 76

Yelverton, Robert de 80
Yelverton, Cecily de, *see under*
  Morley